W9-DDU-131

Activities for
Base Ten Blocks

Sherry Nortman-Wolf
Edited by I.S. Weinzweig, Ph. D.

Contents

Introduction to Base Ten

Manipulatives such as Base Ten Blocks, counters, and bills and coins add another dimension to a child's learning experience. Since every student learns differently, the tactile and visual aspects of manipulatives can help make mathematic concepts concrete for the beginner or the older child. Using manipulatives in the classroom also helps teach skills besides the basic mathematic functions of addition, subtraction, multiplication, and so on. Children also develop their problem-solving, communication, socialization, and reasoning skills. They are able to make connections between the concepts being taught and the world they inhabit.

The exercises in this book are not grade-specific and can be used at any level as a supplement to new material or as a review tool. Activities are grouped by the operations covered in the section. Each page can be photocopied on paper for students and on acetate transparencies for demonstration purposes. The book is intended for use with the Starter Set of Base Ten Blocks (LER 0930)—which includes 100 units, 30 rods, 10 flats, and one cube—or Interlocking Base Ten Blocks Starter Set (LER 6356). Some of the more advanced problems will require more blocks than are provided in the starter set. For those situations, representative drawings of the different types of blocks are printed on the inside back cover of this book. They can be photocopied as often as necessary and distributed to students to make up the required numbers.

Teaching notes are provided for each section in the book. These notes explain how Base Ten Blocks can be used to reinforce important concepts and address common problem areas for students. The terminology used in the teaching notes and exercises is not definitive and may introduce a point of discussion regarding the different ways mathematical concepts can be expressed. For example, *division* may also be called *sharing*; *trading* and *exchanging* may be used instead of *borrowing*, *carrying*, or *regrouping*; *greater than* and *less than* may be *more* and *fewer*.

While children work with the Base Ten Blocks, whether individually or in groups, you will have a chance to observe them and get a genuine feel for their understanding of the various concepts—a type of assessment that isn't always possible with less interactive methods. This book is only a starting point. Use the activities described to create your own games and exercises to stimulate students' interest in and understanding of mathematics.

Base Ten Blocks

Pieces of the Base Ten Blocks are shown below. Can you name them?

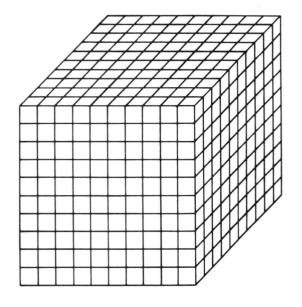

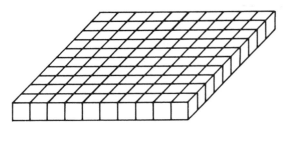

Name: _____

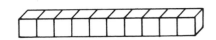

Name: _____

Name: _____

Name: _____

1. Can you find the smallest piece? Put an "S" for "small" next to it.

2. Find the largest piece. Put an "L" for "large" next to it.

3. Find the piece that looks like this: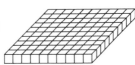
   Put an "X" on it.

4. Now find the piece that looks like this:
   Circle it.

Number and Place Value

Teaching Notes

As students learn about the types of Base Ten Blocks, they will learn to count by ones, tens, hundreds, and thousands. The trading, or exchanging, activities introduce them to the concepts of borrowing and carrying for use in subtraction and addition later.

If you are working with young children who have not seen Base Ten Blocks before, let them explore the different blocks for a while before beginning the activities in this book. Introduce them to each type of block and explain how it will be used.

For older students who have worked with the blocks previously, review basic concepts like place value; ones, tens, and hundreds; and greater than/less than comparisons. Point out how these will be the basis for exercises in other functions such as addition, subtraction, and so on.

As students model numbers using blocks, demonstrate different ways of writing each number—for example, standard form (1,234), expanded form (1,000 + 200 + 30 + 4), and word form (one thousand, two hundred thirty-four). Ask if they know another way to express "one thousand, two hundred" ("twelve hundred").

If students have trouble counting by tens or hundreds, try building walls or structures with rods and flats. Have students count out loud as each layer is added.

Some students have trouble with "greater than" and "less than" symbols. You can demonstrate the correct symbols by putting two groups of units on the overhead projector. Have the class count each group and decide which has fewer units. Put a dot next to that group; the dot signifies the point of the arrow (symbol). Thus, the dot always goes next to the smaller number, and they draw the symbol from that. To reinforce this, you can have students draw in greater than/less than symbols in the activity on page 30 rather than circling the larger number.

Units, Units, Units

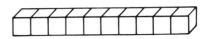

has as many units as

Remember: 10 units have the same value as 1 rod.

See if you can answer the questions below:

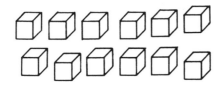

1. How many units are there? _____
   Circle 10 units. Exchange the circled units for one rod.

   You now have _____ rod(s), _____ unit(s).

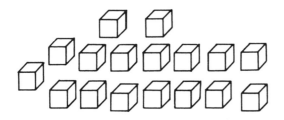

2. How many units are there? _____
   Circle 10 units. Exchange the circled units for one rod.

   You now have _____ rod(s), _____ unit(s).

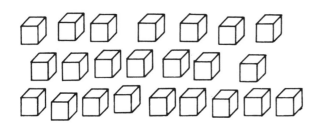

3. How many units are there? _____
   Circle 10 units. Exchange the circled units for one rod.

   You now have _____ rod(s), _____ unit(s).
   Circle another 10 units. Exchange the circled units for one rod.

   You now have _____ rod(s), _____ unit(s).

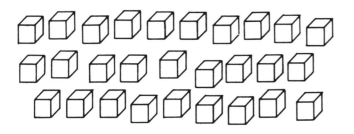

4. How many units are there? _____
   Circle 10 units. Exchange the circled units for one rod.

   You now have _____ rod(s), _____ unit(s).
   Circle another 10 units. Exchange the circled units for one rod.

   You now have _____ rod(s), _____ unit(s).

Units, Units, Units

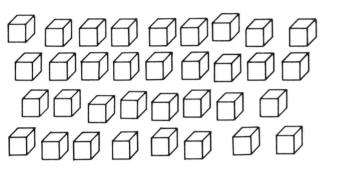

5. How many units are there? _____
   Circle 10 units. Exchange the circled units for one rod.

   You now have _____ rod(s), _____ unit(s).
   Circle another 10 units. Exchange the circled units for one rod.

   You now have _____ rod(s), _____ unit(s).
   Circle another 10 units. Exchange the circled units for one rod.

   You now have _____ rod(s), _____ unit(s).

6. How many units? _____
   Circle 10 units. Exchange the circled units for one rod.

   You now have _____ rod(s), _____ unit(s).
   Circle another 10 units. Exchange the circled units for one rod.

   You now have _____ rod(s), _____ unit(s).
   Circle another 10 units. Exchange the circled units for one rod.

   You now have _____ rod(s), _____ unit(s).

Now It's Your Turn

Try this activity again. This time you choose how many units. Make sure that each time you circle 10 units, you exchange them for one rod.

Remember the questions to ask:

   How many units?
   Circle 10 units, exchange for one rod.

   You now have _____ rod(s), _____ unit(s).
   Can you circle another 10 units?

   If yes, you now have _____ rod(s), _____ unit(s).

Repeat this until you cannot circle any more groups of 10 units.
Keep a record of what you have done.

Trading Rods and Units

Let's start with:

Now we can make a chart to record our progress.

START WITH 16 UNITS

Number of Exchange	Now Have		Total Number of
	Rods	Units	Units Exchanged
1	1	6	10

Remember: Circle 10 units and exchange for 1 rod.

You try it.

Count out the number of units indicated. Make exchanges and record each exchange on the chart.

1. START WITH 33 UNITS

Number of Exchange	Now Have		Total Number of
	Rods	Units	Units Exchanged
1	1	23	10
2	2	13	20

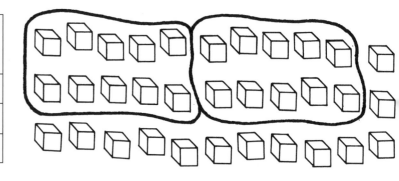

Now do them on your own!

2. START WITH 56 UNITS

Number of Exchange	Now Have		Total Number of
	Rods	Units	Units Exchanged
1			
2			
3			
4			
5			

Trading Rods and Units

3. START WITH 65 UNITS

Number of Exchange	Now Have		Total Number of Units Exchanged
	Rods	Units	

4. START WITH 79 UNITS

Number of Exchange	Now Have		Total Number of Units Exchanged
	Rods	Units	

5. START WITH 87 UNITS

Number of Exchange	Now Have		Total Number of Units Exchanged
	Rods	Units	

6. START WITH 48 UNITS

Number of Exchange	Now Have		Total Number of Units Exchanged
	Rods	Units	

7. START WITH 50 UNITS

Number of Exchange	Now Have		Total Number of Units Exchanged
	Rods	Units	

At the Toy Shop

Pat's Toy Shop is quite unusual. All the toys are made of strangely shaped wood. Each unit is worth one penny; each rod costs one dime. Can you help Pat price these toys?

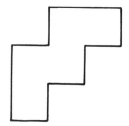

1. How many units can you fit into this shape? _____

   How many rods fit? _____

   How many pennies would this shape cost? _____

   How would you pay for it using the fewest coins?

   _____dime(s), _____pennies

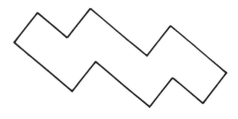

2. How many units can you fit into this shape? _____

   How many rods fit? _____

   How many pennies would this shape cost? _____

   How would you pay for it using the fewest coins?

   _____dime(s), _____pennies

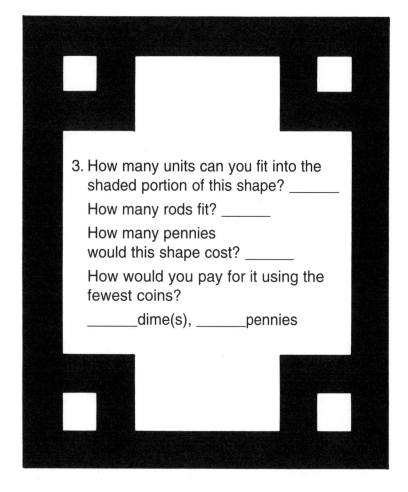

3. How many units can you fit into the shaded portion of this shape? _____

   How many rods fit? _____

   How many pennies would this shape cost? _____

   How would you pay for it using the fewest coins?

   _____dime(s), _____pennies

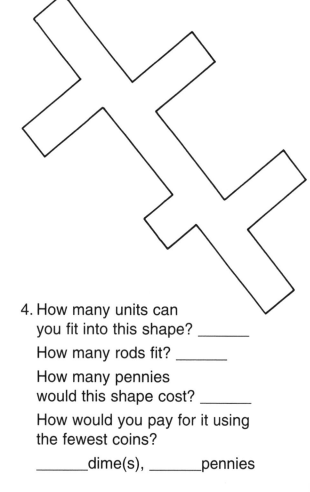

4. How many units can you fit into this shape? _____

   How many rods fit? _____

   How many pennies would this shape cost? _____

   How would you pay for it using the fewest coins?

   _____dime(s), _____pennies

Units and Rods

Helen and Jack were working with units and exchanging them for rods, but they forgot to record all the numbers. Can you help them fill in the rest of the chart?

Units Started With	Total Number of Units Exchanged	Now Have	
		Rods	Units
16	10	1	6
38	30	3	8
54			
47			
	60		7
		8	3
90			
	40		6
85			
		9	3
79			

Let's Roll for It!

This game is for three to five players. Ask your teacher for a die and a collection of units and rods.

Each person should roll the die. The person with the highest roll goes first. The person with the lowest roll should be the banker.

Each player rolls the die and the banker gives him or her the number of units indicated on the die. As soon as possible, trade for 1 rod. (You must make the exchange as soon as possible.) If another player catches you with more than 10 units in your pile, all of the units from your last roll must be returned to the banker.

The first player to get 5 rods wins!

Want to make it more difficult? Try these variations:

1. You must figure out the exchange as soon as the die is rolled, and tell the other players *before* you can collect from the bank.
2. To win, you must get *exactly* 5 rods. So, if you have 4 rods and 6 units and then roll a 5, you must forfeit your turn.

Keep It Rolling

It takes 10 units to make a rod. You collect units by rolling a die and taking the number of units indicated on the die.

For example, if is rolled, you would receive 4 units.

1. What is the smallest number you could roll? _____

2. What is the largest number you could roll? _____

3. If you wanted exactly one rod, what is the smallest number of rolls you could make? _____
   Give two examples of combinations you could roll to do this. _____ _____ or _____ _____.
   Are there any other rolls that would make this possible? _____

4. If you wanted exactly one rod, what is the most rolls you would have to make? _____
   What number would you have to roll each time if this happened? _____

5. If it took 3 rolls to get a rod, what could you have rolled? _____ _____ _____

6. What about 4 rolls? _____ _____ _____ _____

7. What about 5 rolls? _____ _____ _____ _____ _____

Counting Backward

Sam challenged Helen to a duel. He claimed that she couldn't count backward, exchanging rods for units. Helen thought that she could. Help her prove Sam wrong.

Here is a sample:

START WITH 6 RODS, 5 UNITS

Number of Exchange	Total Number of Rods Exchanged	Now Have	
		Rods	Units
1	1	5	15
2	2	4	25
3	3	3	35
4	4	2	45
5	5	1	55
6	6	0	65

Now you try!

1. START WITH 5 RODS, 8 UNITS

Number of Exchange	Total Number of Rods Exchanged	Now Have	
		Rods	Units

2. START WITH 4 RODS, 9 UNITS

Number of Exchange	Total Number of Rods Exchanged	Now Have	
		Rods	Units

Counting Backward

3. START WITH 7 RODS, 1 UNIT

Number of Exchange	Total Number of Rods Exchanged	Now Have	
		Rods	Units

4. START WITH 6 RODS, 0 UNITS

Number of Exchange	Total Number of Rods Exchanged	Now Have	
		Rods	Units

5. START WITH 8 RODS, 3 UNITS

Number of Exchange	Total Number of Rods Exchanged	Now Have	
		Rods	Units

Meet the Flat

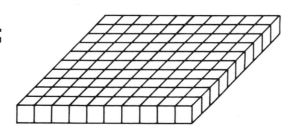

This piece is called a flat.
Can you find a block that looks like it? Draw its outline in the space below.

1. Does a rod fit inside the outline? _____
   How many rods are needed to fill the shape? _____

2. You have filled the shape with rods. Therefore,
   1 flat has the same value as _____ rods. If you
   exchange 1 rod for units, you will have _____ rods,
   _____ units. If you exchange a second rod for units,
   you will have _____ rods, _____ units.

3. Start with 1 flat, which has the same value as
   _____ rods. Now complete this chart:

4. From your chart, you see that 1 flat has the same
   value as _____ rods. Also, 1 flat is equivalent
   to _____ units.

Total Number of Rods Exchanged	Now Have	
	Rods	Units

Let's Make a Trade

Start with:

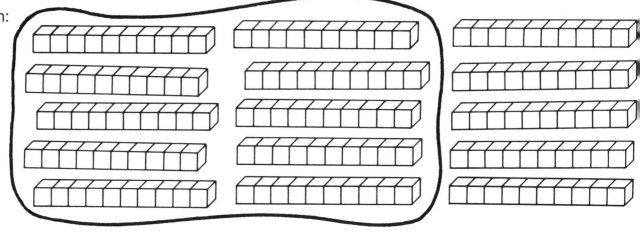

Let's make a chart.

START WITH 15 RODS

Number of Exchange	Now Have		Total Number of Rods Exchanged
	Flats	Rods	
1	1	5	10

Remember: Circle 10 rods; trade for 1 flat.

You try! Count out a starting number of rods. Then make the necessary exchanges and record your response on the charts. The first one is started for you.

1. START WITH 22 RODS

Number of Exchange	Now Have		Total Number of Rods Exchanged
	Flats	Rods	
1	1	12	10

Let's Make a Trade

2. START WITH 63 RODS

Number of Exchange	Now Have		Total Number of Rods Exchanged
	Flats	Rods	

3. START WITH 71 RODS

Number of Exchange	Now Have		Total Number of Rods Exchanged
	Flats	Rods	

4. START WITH 89 RODS

Number of Exchange	Now Have		Total Number of Rods Exchanged
	Flats	Rods	

5. START WITH 45 RODS

Number of Exchange	Now Have		Total Number of Rods Exchanged
	Flats	Rods	

6. START WITH 50 RODS

Number of Exchange	Now Have		Total Number of Rods Exchanged
	Flats	Rods	

Trading Practice

Remember: 10 units have the same value as 1 rod. 10 rods are equivalent to 1 flat.

Let's do some more exchanges. The first chart has been filled in for you.

START WITH 134 UNITS

Number of Exchange	Now Have			Total Number of Units Exchanged	Total Number of Rods Exchanged
	Flats	Rods	Units		
1	0	1	124	10	0
2	0	2	114	20	0
3	0	3	104	30	0
4	0	4	94	40	0
5	0	5	84	50	0
6	0	6	74	60	0
7	0	7	64	70	0
8	0	8	54	80	0
9	0	9	44	90	0
10	0	10	34	100	0
11	1	0	34	110	10
12	1	1	24	120	10
13	1	2	14	130	10
14	1	3	4	130	10

Now you try it! As you make your exchanges, check to see if a pattern develops. Use it to help you.

Trading Practice

START WITH 256 UNITS

Number of Exchange	Now Have			Total Number of Units Exchanged	Total Number of Rods Exchanged
	Flats	Rods	Units		
1					
2					
3					
4					
5					
6					
7					
8					
9					
10					
11					
12					
13					
14					
15					
16					
17					
18					
19					
20					
21					
22					
23					
24					
25					
26					
27					

Number Patterns

After completing several charts, Pete noticed certain patterns.

For example:

If he started with 257 units and exchanged those for rods, he ended up with 25 rods, 7 units.
If the rods were then exchanged for flats, he had 2 flats, 5 rods, 7 units.

He reasoned that if he started with 362 units, he would end up with 3 flats, 6 rods, and 2 units.

Help Pete confirm his theory by filling in the spaces below:

Number of Units to Start With	Exchange for Rods Now Have		Exchange for Flats Now Have		
	Rods	Units	Flats	Rods	Units
275					
463					
782					
603					
526					
419					
378					
487					
136					
283					

Which exchange allows you to state the value of the block using the fewest number of pieces?

_____

Save the Day!

Eddie decided to be helpful by erasing all of the answers Susan had filled in on the chart below. Luckily, he left some spaces untouched. Can you help figure out what should go in the empty spaces?

Number of Units	Total Number of Units Exchanged	Total Number of Rods Exchanged	Now Have		
			Flats	Rods	Units
35	30	0	0	3	5
235	230	20	2	3	5
143					
367					7
	450				0
			5	4	9
307					
	630				0
98					
			1	8	2
	40				3
596					

Conversions

Look at the number of units shown in Column 1. How would the other columns be filled out if you had done all the exchanges you could for each number? Record the results below. The first one has been done for you.

Number of Units	Flats	Rods	Units
45	0	4	5
99			
35			
321			
903			
400			
563			
89			
657			
835			
198			
387			
742			
946			
849			

Meet the Cube

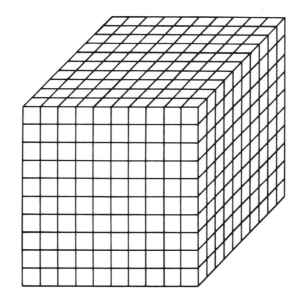

This piece is called a cube. Can you find a block that looks like it? Set it down in front of you.

1. Place a flat on top of the cube. Does it fit exactly? _____

2. Place the flat next to the cube and stack more flats on top.
   How many flats must be stacked to reach the same height as the cube? _____
   Therefore, we can say that _____ flats have the same value as _____ cube.

3. If you exchanged one of the flats that make up a cube for rods,
   you would have _____ flats, _____ rods.

Keep exchanging the flats for rods. Complete this chart as you go:

Number of Flats Exchanged	Now Have	
	Flats	Rods
1		

4. Thus, we can say that 1 cube has the same value as _____ flats,
   and that one cube is equivalent to _____ rods.

Exchanging Flats

Start with:

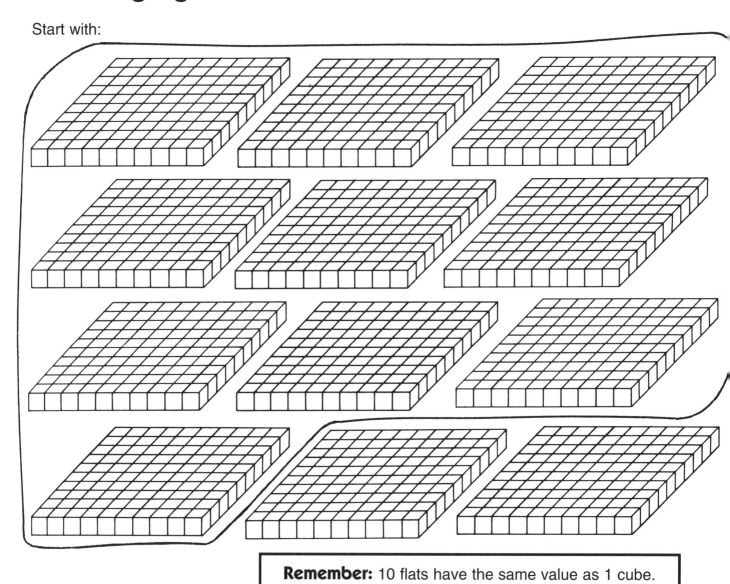

Remember: 10 flats have the same value as 1 cube.

START WITH 12 FLATS

Number of Exchange	Now Have		Total Number of Flats Exchanged
	Cubes	Flats	
1	1	2	10

Now you try. Make exchanges and record each exchange on the chart.

1. START WITH 24 FLATS

Number of Exchange	Now Have		Total Number of Flats Exchanged
	Cubes	Flats	

24

Exchanging Flats

2. START WITH 67 FLATS

Number of Exchange	Now Have		Total Number of Flats Exchanged
	Cubes	Flats	

3. START WITH 39 FLATS

Number of Exchange	Now Have		Total Number of Flats Exchanged
	Cubes	Flats	

4. START WITH 81 FLATS

Number of Exchange	Now Have		Total Number of Flats Exchanged
	Cubes	Flats	

5. START WITH 48 FLATS

Number of Exchange	Now Have		Total Number of Flats Exchanged
	Cubes	Flats	

6. START WITH 53 FLATS

Number of Exchange	Now Have		Total Number of Flats Exchanged
	Cubes	Flats	

7. START WITH 70 FLATS

Number of Exchange	Now Have		Total Number of Flats Exchanged
	Cubes	Flats	

Let's Trade

Remember: 10 flats have the same value as 1 cube. 10 rods are equivalent to 1 flat.

Study the chart.
Do any patterns exist?
Use them to help you
make exchanges.

START WITH 119 RODS

Number of Exchange	Now Have			Total Number of Units Exchanged	Total Number of Rods Exchanged
	Flats	Rods	Units		
1	0	1	109	10	0
2	0	2	99	20	0
3	0	3	89	30	0
4	0	4	79	40	0
5	0	5	69	50	0
6	0	6	59	60	0
7	0	7	49	70	0
8	0	8	39	80	0
9	0	9	29	90	0
10	0	10	19	100	0
11	1	10	19	100	0
12	1	1	9	110	10

Now you try!

START WITH 135 RODS

Number of Exchange	Now Have			Total Number of Units Exchanged	Total Number of Rods Exchanged
	Flats	Rods	Units		

Erased!

In his eagerness to help, Eddie has done it again! He has erased almost all the answers Susan had filled in on the chart below. Lucky for you, he was caught before he finished.

Help figure out what should go in the empty spaces.

Number of Rods Started With	Total Number of Rods Exchanged	Total Number of Flats Exchanged	Now Have		
			Cubes	Flats	Rods
46	40	0	0	4	6
324	320	30	3	2	4
234					
278					
	360				8
			6	3	7
506					
	740				0
			2	7	3
	50				4
			5	9	6
458					

Complete the Chart

Jason studied all the charts you have carefully completed. He observed certain patterns occurring.

If he started with 1,234 units and exchanged as many rods as he could, there would be 123 rods, 4 units. If he then traded the rods for as many flats as he could, he would have 12 flats, 3 rods, 4 units. Finally, if he traded the flats for cubes, he would have 1 cube, 2 flats, 3 rods, 4 units.

It was clear to him that the same value could be given in many different ways, depending on the number of pieces used.

Let's put his idea to work by filling in the chart below:

Start with this number of units	Exchange for Rods Now Have		Exchange for Flats Now Have			Exchange for Cubes Now Have			
	Rods	Units	Flats	Rods	Units	Cubes	Flats	Rods	Units
1,364									
2,375									
1,693									
2,390									
3,457									
1,409									
4,372									
2,437									
634									
4,361									

Construct These Numbers

Look at the numbers of units in Column 1. If you exchanged as many blocks as you could for each number, what would you end up with? Record your results in the chart below. The first one has been completed for you.

Number of Units	Cubes	Flats	Rods	Units
1,345	1	3	4	5
299				
3,275				
1,321				
804				
3,700				
2,654				
498				
1,078				
3,568				
924				
1,196				
2,837				
2,310				
3,247				

Greater Than, Less Than, or Equal To?

For each of the following problems, circle the group of blocks that is greater than the other. If the two groups are equal, write an equal sign (=) between them. The first problem has been done for you.

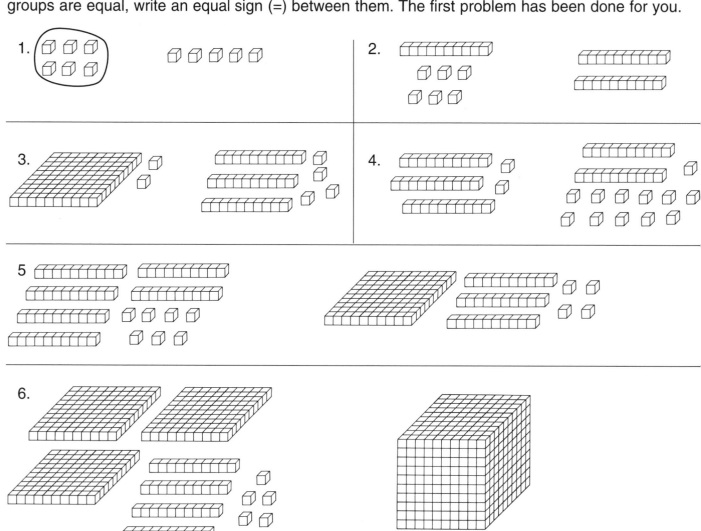

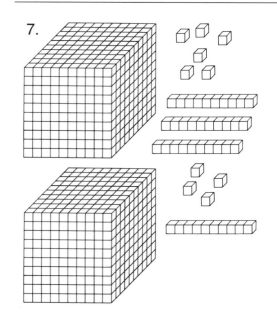

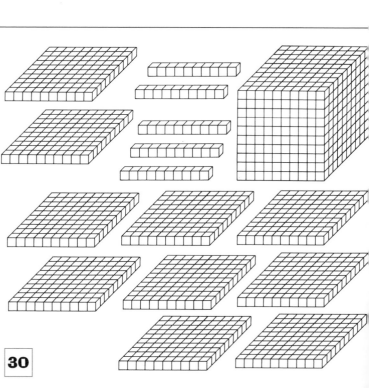

Addition

Teaching Notes

Base Ten Blocks can be used to illustrate the different properties of addition: commutative (1 + 2 = 2 + 1); zero (0 + 4 = 4); and associative ([1 + 3] + 9 = 1 + [3 + 9]).

Make the connection between place value and addition—when we add numbers together, we have to know how to trade or regroup them by ones, tens, and so on. The "Combining Collections" exercises can help emphasize this. Translate students' work with blocks to lining up digits in addition problems on the blackboard or overhead projector.

When adding three- or four-digit numbers, some students may begin at the left instead of the right. Have them draw a red star next to the heading of the Units column in the charts (or the Ones column on the place value mat) to remind them where to begin.

If students are having trouble adding more than two numbers and you want to show them that $(x + y) + z$ is the same as $x + (y + z)$, divide the class into pairs or groups. Write an addition problem on the blackboard (for example, 12 + 45 + 120 + 6). Have students construct each number, then come up with a way of grouping them (such as 12 + 45 and 6 + 120) before adding them all together and making exchanges. Write each group's method on the blackboard and show that they all produce the same sum.

All in the Bottom

Look at the number of unit blocks in the first rectangle.
Now look at the number of unit blocks in the second rectangle.
Place unit blocks over the pictures on this page. If you combine all the pieces and move them to the bottom rectangle, how many will you have in all?

The first one is started for you.

1.

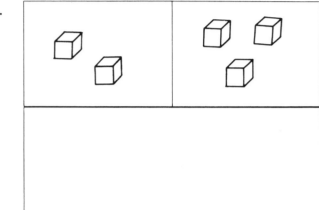

Think: 2   in 1st box ⟶

3   in 2nd box

5   in all   ⟶

2	3
5	

2.

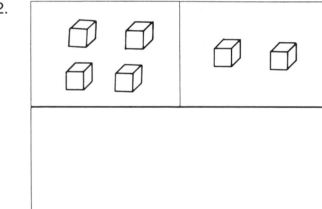

Think: _____ in 1st box ⟶

_____ in 2nd box

_____ in all ⟶

3.

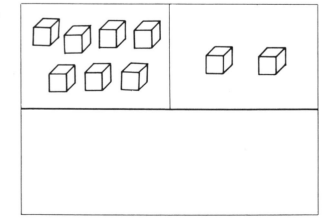

Think: _____ in 1st box

_____ in 2nd box

_____ in all

Fact Rectangles

Let's make it a little more difficult. The rectangles below are called fact rectangles.

Look at the number of units in the first rectangle. Record the number in the space provided. Do the same for the second rectangle. If you move all the units into the bottom rectangle, how many would you have?

1.

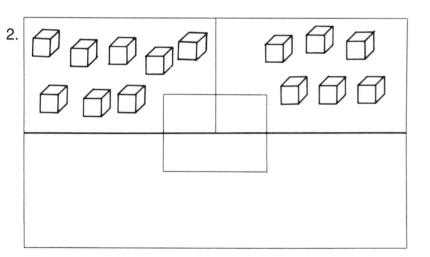

Can you exchange any units for rods?
If so, _____ rod(s), _____ unit(s).

2.

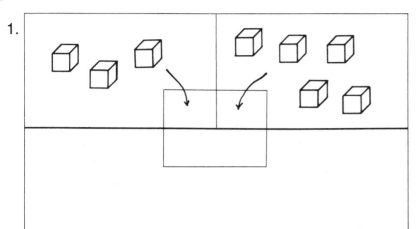

Can you exchange any units for rods?
If so, _____ rod(s), _____ unit(s).

3.

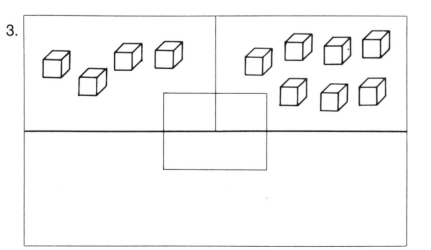

Can you exchange any units for rods?
If so, _____ rod(s), _____ unit(s).

Combine Collections

Kyle and Ashley were working together. Kyle reached into a bucket of blocks and pulled out 3 cubes, 4 flats, 13 rods, and 12 units. He made the exchanges necessary to get the same value using the fewest blocks and recorded the results in the chart below. Ashley then reached in and pulled out 1 cube, 15 flats, 6 rods, and 14 units. She also made exchanges and recorded her results.

Let's look at these:

	Cubes	Flats	Rods	Units
Kyle	3	5	4	2
Ashley	2	5	7	4
Total	5	10	11	6
Exchanges	1	1		
Total After Exchange	6	1	1	6

They decided to combine their collections.

They made some exchanges to show the same value using the fewest pieces.

Let's do it again.
Look at what Kyle and Ashley have picked.
Pick out the same blocks from your own collection.
Figure out the total, then exchange blocks for the same value, using the fewest pieces.

	Cubes	Flats	Rods	Units
Kyle	1	4	6	3
Ashley	3	8	2	7
Total				
Exchanges				
Total After Exchange				

Combining the Blocks

For this activity, you need two students to duplicate the game played by Kyle and Ashley on page 34.

Let's review the steps:
1. Student A goes to the collection box and (with eyes closed) picks out blocks.
2. He or she makes any exchanges necessary to represent the amount picked using the fewest pieces.
3. Student A records the amount in the chart provided.
4. Student B performs Steps 1, 2, and 3.
5. Student A and Student B now see how many blocks they have in all.
6. They make exchanges to represent the amount using the fewest pieces.

Do this activity 10 times. Share your solutions with your teacher when you have completed them.

1.

Name	Cubes	Flats	Rods	Units
Total				
Exchanges				
Total After Exchange				

2.

Name	Cubes	Flats	Rods	Units
Total				
Exchanges				
Total After Exchange				

3.

Name	Cubes	Flats	Rods	Units
Total				
Exchanges				
Total After Exchange				

4.

Name	Cubes	Flats	Rods	Units
Total				
Exchanges				
Total After Exchange				

Want a Challenge?
Try this activity with three or four students together.

Check the Totals

Kyle and Ashley had a lot of fun putting their collections together to see how many they had in all. The results of their collections and the totals are below. Check to see if the Total After Exchange row is correct for each problem. If they are not, show what should be changed.

1.

Name	Cubes	Flats	Rods	Units
Kyle	2	7	9	8
Ashley	3	8	6	5
Total	5	15	15	13
Total After Exchange	5	6	5	3

Record any corrections needed here:

Cubes	Flats	Rods	Units

2.

Name	Cubes	Flats	Rods	Units
Kyle	3	4	5	2
Ashley	5	6	4	8
Total	8	10	9	10
Total After Exchange	8	1	0	0

Record any corrections needed here:

Cubes	Flats	Rods	Units

3.

Name	Cubes	Flats	Rods	Units
Kyle	2	5	7	4
Ashley	4	9	3	8
Total	6	14	10	12
Total After Exchange	7	5	1	2

Record any corrections needed here:

Cubes	Flats	Rods	Units

Find the Total

Let's look at more of Kyle's and Ashley's record sheets. This time, you total them and make any exchanges necessary to represent the value using the fewest pieces.

1.

Name	Cubes	Flats	Rods	Units
Kyle	5	7	9	6
Ashley	2	4	7	8
Total				
Total After Exchange				

2.

Name	Cubes	Flats	Rods	Units
Kyle	3	1	6	8
Ashley	5	7	3	9
Total				
Total After Exchange				

3.

Name	Cubes	Flats	Rods	Units
Kyle	4	5	9	7
Ashley	1	8	6	4
Total				
Total After Exchange				

4.

Name	Cubes	Flats	Rods	Units
Kyle	3	1	8	4
Ashley	6	2	3	5
Total				
Total After Exchange				

Practice Combining the Blocks

On the next few pages are copies of students' record sheets. See if you can figure out how many blocks each student has, and make the exchanges necessary to represent the value using the fewest pieces.

1.

	Cubes	Flats	Rods	Units
	3	6	9	4
	2	8	5	7
Total				
Total After Exchange				

2.

	Cubes	Flats	Rods	Units
	3	5	7	6
	2	3	4	9
Total				
Total After Exchange				

3.

	Cubes	Flats	Rods	Units
	6	5	8	7
	2	4	8	6
Total				
Total After Exchange				

4.

	Cubes	Flats	Rods	Units
	5	3	7	6
	3	6	1	5
Total				
Total After Exchange				

5.

	Cubes	Flats	Rods	Units
	7	8	4	6
	1	8	4	6
Total				
Total After Exchange				

6.

	Cubes	Flats	Rods	Units
	6	3	9	2
	1	5	4	7
Total				
Total After Exchange				

More Practice Combining the Blocks

1.

	Cubes	Flats	Rods	Units
	5	7	6	8
	3	1	2	4
Total				
Total After Exchange				

2.

	Cubes	Flats	Rods	Units
	3	9	8	5
	2	4	6	7
Total				
Total After Exchange				

3.

	Cubes	Flats	Rods	Units
	8	2	8	5
	1	3	9	5
Total				
Total After Exchange				

4.

	Cubes	Flats	Rods	Units
	4	9	7	4
	3	8	7	6
Total				
Total After Exchange				

5.

	Cubes	Flats	Rods	Units
	6	7	9	3
	4	8	2	6
Total				
Total After Exchange				

6.

	Cubes	Flats	Rods	Units
	5	8	6	1
	4	7	3	9
Total				
Total After Exchange				

Addition Practice

Here are more problems. Ashley and Kyle got tired and left off the headings. However, you should still find the total by making the exchanges necessary to represent the value using the fewest pieces. The first one is done for you.

	3	6	5	4
	2	8	7	3
	1	1	1	
	6	5	2	7

1.
2	8	3	5
5	9	6	8

2.
7	9	8	4
1	8	9	7

3.
3	8	4	6
2	6	9	7

4.
8	7	4	6
1	2	4	8

5.
4	6	7	8
5	8	9	6

6.
5	3	4	0
2	9	4	7

7.
3	4	0	5
8	9	4	5

8.
4	1	8	6
6	8	3	6

Subtraction

Teaching Notes

The "Don't Go Broke!" exercises in this section reinforce both subtraction and addition principles and give students a chance to use problem-solving skills as they determine which operation to use. Emphasize the link between addition and subtraction (that is, $x + y = z$, so $z - x = y$). Show students how they can verify the answer to a subtraction problem by adding blocks together. Students should also be aware that they may need to exchange rods for units, flats for rods, or even cubes for flats in the "Don't Go Broke!" exercises, if they do not have enough to give away.

Both place value and an understanding of greater than/less than are important for subtraction. Use the "Borrowing" exercise to reinforce that we always subtract from a greater number, so if there are not enough ones, we need to borrow (regroup). When subtracting three- or four-digit numbers, some students may begin at the left instead of the right. Have them draw a red star next to the heading of the Units column in the charts (or the Ones column on the place value mat) to remind them where to begin.

Don't Go Broke!

Jeff and Liz have invented a new game.

They have made a spinner that looks like this:

The game begins by spinning the spinner and rolling a pair of dice. (One red die represents the number of rods. One white die represents units.) If the spinner lands on "Give," the player gives the number of rods and units indicated on the dice to the other player. If the spinner lands on "Take," the player takes the number of rods and units indicated on the dice from the other player. If the spinner points to "Bank," the player gives the amount of the dice roll back to the Bank.

Each player starts with 10 rods and keeps a record of each turn. The first player to run out of units loses. Remember, you can get more units by exchanging one of your rods.

Let's look at Jeff's record sheet for his first five turns.

Spin 1—GIVE

	Rods	Units
Started	10	
Give	6	3
Left	3	7

Spin 2—TAKE

	Rods	Units
Started	3	7
Take	5	6
Left	9	3

Spin 3—BANK

	Rods	Units
Started	9	3
Bank	4	2
Left	5	1

Spin 4—GIVE

	Rods	Units
Started	5	1
Give	3	6
Left	1	5

Spin 5—TAKE

	Rods	Units
Started	1	5
Take	6	4
Left	7	9

Now see if you can figure out Liz's moves.

Spin 1—BANK

	Rods	Units
Started	10	
Bank	3	2
Left		

Spin 2—GIVE

	Rods	Units
Started		
Give	1	6
Left		

Spin 3—TAKE

	Rods	Units
Started		
Take	5	3
Left		

Spin 4—GIVE

	Rods	Units
Started		
Give	4	6
Left		

Spin 5—BANK

	Rods	Units
Started		
Bank	4	3
Left		

If you did everything correctly, Liz should have 1 rod, 6 units left.

More "Don't Go Broke!"

Liz and Jeff decided to play until one of them ran out of rods. Let's see if you can figure out the results of each spin.

JEFF

Spin 6—BANK

	Rods	Units
Started	7	9
Bank	3	6
Left		

Spin 7—TAKE

	Rods	Units
Started		
Take	2	6
Left		

Spin 8—BANK

	Rods	Units
Started		
Bank	4	4
Left		

Spin 9—GIVE

	Rods	Units
Started		
Give	3	1
Left		

LIZ

Spin 6—TAKE

	Rods	Units
Started	1	6
Take	4	5
Left		

Spin 7—TAKE

	Rods	Units
Started		
Take	3	1
Left		

Spin 8—GIVE

	Rods	Units
Started		
Give	2	4
Left		

Spin 9—BANK

	Rods	Units
Started		
Bank	1	6
Left		

Spin 9 caused someone to go broke. Who was it? _____

43

Don't Go Flat Broke!

Liz and Jeff really enjoyed the new game and decided to expand on it. They kept the spinner they had been using, but added three spinners, numbered 1 through 9 to represent units, rods, and flats. They gave themselves 9 flats, 9 rods, and 9 units each to start.

Remember: You can exchange flats for more rods and rods for more units.

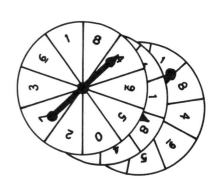

Let's see what Liz's first two spins were:

Spin 1—BANK

	Flats	Rods	Units
Started	9	9	9
Bank	6	4	5
Left	3	5	4

Spin 2—TAKE

	Flats	Rods	Units
Started	3	5	4
Take	5	6	9
Left	9	2	3

Now figure the results for her next two spins.

Spin 3—GIVE

	Flats	Rods	Units
Started	9	2	3
Give	3	8	1
Left			

Spin 4—TAKE

	Flats	Rods	Units
Started			
Take	2	5	7
Left			

Let's take a look at some other rolls. You fill in the results.

1.

Jeff	Flats	Rods	Units
Started	8	5	2
Bank	3	7	4
Left			

2.

Liz	Flats	Rods	Units
Started	6	4	8
Give	5	9	3
Left			

3.

Jeff	Flats	Rods	Units
Started	3	8	5
Take	4	3	7
Left			

4.

Liz	Flats	Rods	Units
Started	5	8	1
Bank	3	7	9
Left			

Raising the Stakes

Liz and Jeff wanted to see what would happen if they expanded their game to include cubes. They knew that they really couldn't collect or give away cubes because they didn't have enough pieces. So they decided to use strips of paper to represent the 9 cubes they wanted to start with. They used four spinners, numbered 0 through 9 to represent the units, rods, flats, and cubes, as well as the action spinner. They each started with 9 cubes, 9 flats, 9 rods, and 9 units.

Let's see what Jeff's first two spins were like:

Spin 1—GIVE

	Cubes	Flats	Rods	Units
Started	9	9	9	9
Give	5	4	6	8
Left	4	5	3	1

Spin 2—TAKE

	Cubes	Flats	Rods	Units
Started	4	5	3	1
Take	4	6	7	8
Left	9	2	0	9

You figure the results for his next two spins.

Spin 3—BANK

	Cubes	Flats	Rods	Units
Started	9	2	0	9
Bank	4	1	3	7
Left				

Spin 4—TAKE

	Cubes	Flats	Rods	Units
Started				
Take	3	2	6	8
Left				

Look at some other rolls, and record the results.

1.

Jeff	Cubes	Flats	Rods	Units
Started	6	9	6	3
Bank	4	4	8	5
Left				

2.

Liz	Cubes	Flats	Rods	Units
Started	7	5	3	7
Give	4	4	8	2
Left				

3.

Jeff	Cubes	Flats	Rods	Units
Started	7	4	9	6
Take	2	5	4	8
Left				

4.

Liz	Cubes	Flats	Rods	Units
Started	5	6	9	2
Give	4	4	8	9
Left				

Borrowing

Liz approached Jeff with a suggestion:

"Jeff, instead of copying your records over and over, how about making your exchanges right above your original value. Let me show you what I mean!"

	Cubes	Flats	Rods	Units
	4	12	11	16
Start	5̶	3̶	2̶	6̶
Give	2	4	5	9

"You need to make exchanges for flats, rods, and units. Think about what the exchange will be and record it above the amount you started with. Notice there are not enough units or rods or flats, so we exchange 1 cube, leaving us with 4, which we enter above 5. Now we have 13 flats, but we need to exchange one of these so we enter a 12 above 3 in the flats column. This gives us 12 rods, but we need to exchange one of these for units. We enter 11 above the 2 in the rods column and 16 above the 6 in units. We still have the same value, but now we have enough of each piece to give away."

"Here, you try it. Just make the necessary exchanges. But be careful! Sometimes an exchange will not be necessary. For example, look at this chart."

	Cubes	Flats	Rods	Units
	3	13	5	13
Start	4̶	3̶	6̶	3̶
Give	1	8	5	6

1.

	Cubes	Flats	Rods	Units
Start	6	7	6	5
Give	4	3	9	7

2.

	Cubes	Flats	Rods	Units
Start	5	3	7	0
Give	4	8	9	4

3.

	Cubes	Flats	Rods	Units
Start	5	3	7	1
Give	4	8	4	9

4.

	Cubes	Flats	Rods	Units
Start	4	0	3	0
Give	2	2	8	7

5.

	Cubes	Flats	Rods	Units
Start	7	6	5	4
Give	4	9	6	8

6.

	Cubes	Flats	Rods	Units
Start	6	5	0	4
Give	2	9	3	8

7.

	Cubes	Flats	Rods	Units
Start	8	9	2	0
Give	3	6	5	1

8.

	Cubes	Flats	Rods	Units
Start	7	4	8	6
Give	3	6	8	9

What Remains

Try using Liz's technique to find out what remains. Notice Liz uses minus signs (−) to indicate that she wants to give away the bottom amount.

The first one has been completed for you.

1.

Cubes	Flats	Rods	Units
5	6	15	14
5	7	6	4
− 3	5	8	6
2	1	7	8

2.

Cubes	Flats	Rods	Units
8	6	4	3
− 5	7	8	2

3.

Cubes	Flats	Rods	Units
7	5	7	3
− 3	6	7	7

4.

Cubes	Flats	Rods	Units
6	0	7	4
− 4	8	5	8

5.

Cubes	Flats	Rods	Units
6	7	0	7
− 4	8	9	4

6.

Cubes	Flats	Rods	Units
7	2	6	5
− 5	3	9	8

7.

Cubes	Flats	Rods	Units
5	7	0	0
− 4	3	8	2

8.

Cubes	Flats	Rods	Units
8	0	7	6
− 6	2	7	8

9.

Cubes	Flats	Rods	Units
4	0	4	7
− 2	9	3	8

10.

Cubes	Flats	Rods	Units
5	3	0	5
− 3	8	4	5

Find the Value

Andy came along and challenged Jeff and Liz to find out how much was left. He used a minus sign (–) to tell them to "give" the bottom amount.

1.
```
    6 6 7 5
  − 4 5 9 7
```

2.
```
    7 7 5 4
  − 4 8 6 3
```

3.
```
    8 6 8 4
  − 4 7 8 6
```

4.
```
    5 0 6 4
  − 3 7 3 7
```

5.
```
    5 6 0 8
  − 2 7 3 5
```

6.
```
    6 3 7 6
  − 3 4 8 9
```

7.
```
    7 8 0 0
  − 3 4 6 7
```

8.
```
    7 0 9 3
  − 5 3 6 8
```

9.
```
    4 0 5 7
  − 2 3 6 8
```

10.
```
    9 4 0 4
  − 4 8 6 4
```

Multiplication

Teaching Notes

Use Base Ten Blocks to review the properties of multiplication: commutative (4 x 3 = 3 x 4); zero (0 x 6 = 0); associative ([5 x 2] x 6 = 5 x [2 x 6]); and property of one (1 x 9 = 9). Explain how these properties make multiplication easier.

Arrays can help students visualize multiplication problems. Before completing "Multiplying by 10, 100, and 1,000," show students how to set up arrays for simple numbers using units on the overhead projector. For example, for 4 x 3, you would line up four rows of three units each. (You can show the commutative property by rearranging the units to illustrate 3 x 4.)

Let's Multiply

"If you can add, you can multiply," Katie told her friend Alex.

"Are you sure?" Alex asked.

"Sure. We just use the place value mat like we did in addition," Katie replied. "Watch."

Katie took the multiplication problem 7 x 6. She put 7 arrays, or groups, of 6 units in the Ones column of her place value mat. It looked like this:

HUNDREDS	TENS	ONES
		▪▪▪
		▪▪▪
		▪▪▪
		▪▪▪
		▪▪▪
		▪▪▪
		▪▪▪

Next, she combined the units and exchanged as many as she could for rods.

HUNDREDS	TENS	ONES
	IIII	▪ ▪

Her final answer was 4 rods, 2 units, or 42. So, 7 x 6 = 42.

"Wow, that's easy!" said Alex. "Let's do some more."

Next, they tried the problem 13 x 8. Their arrays looked like this:

HUNDREDS	TENS	ONES
	I	▪▪▪
	I	▪▪▪
	I	▪▪▪
	I	▪▪▪
	I	▪▪▪
	I	▪▪▪
	I	▪▪▪
	I	▪▪▪

By trading units for rods and rods for flats, they found they had 1 flat, 0 rods, 4 units, or 104. So, 13 x 8 = 104.

Using your blocks and place value mat, can you help Katie and Alex find the product, or answer, to these problems?

1. 　　5
　　x　3
　　―――――

2. 　1 2
　　x　　8
　　―――――

3. 　2 5
　　x　　6
　　―――――

4. 　5 0
　　x　　4
　　―――――

5. 1 3 4
　　x　　7
　　―――――

6. 3 5 1
　　x　　2
　　―――――

7. 　4 4
　　x　1 9
　　―――――

8. 　7 8
　　x　1 1
　　―――――

Multiplying by 10, 100, and 1,000

These are some of the easiest numbers to multiply by. Let's see how it works with rods, or tens. If you have 14 rods (or 14 x 10), you can exchange 10 of the rods for 1 flat.

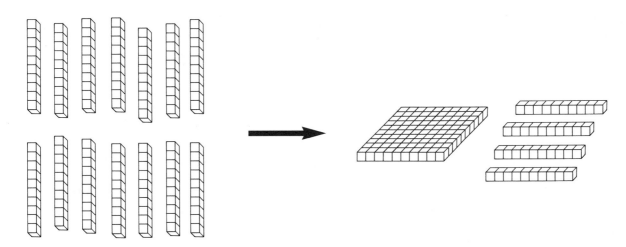

You are left with 1 flat, 4 rods (or 140).

Let's try it with flats, or hundreds. If you have 11 flats (or 11 x 100), you can exchange 10 flats for 1 cube. You are left with 1 cube, 1 flat (or 1,100).

See if you can figure out these multiplication problems using blocks.

1.
$$\begin{array}{r} 1\,0 \\ \times\quad 7 \\ \hline \end{array}$$

2.
$$\begin{array}{r} 4\,5 \\ \times\quad 1\,0 \\ \hline \end{array}$$

3.
$$\begin{array}{r} 1\,0\,0 \\ \times\quad 2\,4 \\ \hline \end{array}$$

4.
$$\begin{array}{r} 1{,}0\,0\,0 \\ \times\quad 2 \\ \hline \end{array}$$

5. Do you see a pattern emerging? Can you think of a shortcut to multiplying with 10, 100, and 1,000? _____

Multiplying with Pete

Pete said to Alex, "Your way of multiplying is okay, but I know a different way to do the same thing."

Pete's method has a code.
These symbols are used to represent each of the blocks:

.　 = unit

——　= rod

☐　= flat

▱ =cube

Using blocks, lay the equivalent of your first number end to end vertically. For the number you want to multiply by, line up a horizontal row of blocks equivalent to that number. Now put a line along the side and the top, as shown below, to create a space for your answer. You can make the line with masking tape on your desk, or you can draw it on a piece of blank paper. Your answer will appear inside this boxed area.

Let's try the first one together.

Say you're given an outline like this:

Now, fill in the pattern as shown:

You have 6 flats, 12 rods, 6 units or 7 flats, 2 rods, 6 units.

You try it!

1.

_____ flats, _____ rods, _____ units

52

Multiplying with Pete

2.

_____ flats, _____ rods, _____ units

3.

_____ flats, _____ rods, _____ units

4.

_____ flats, _____ rods, _____ units

Division

Teaching Notes

Division is presented as the sharing of blocks among a certain number of people. Emphasize the link between multiplication and division (that is, $x \times y = z$, so $z \div x = y$). Show students how they can verify the answer to a division problem by using multiplication.

Talk about how there is sometimes a remainder after division is complete. The remainders should always be less than the divisor. When using Base Ten Blocks to model division, students should choose a specific place on their work area that is for remainder (leftover) units.

If students have trouble with "Division Basics," reinforce the main concepts by writing on the overhead projector and constructing a number with Base Ten Blocks, for example 225 (2 flats, 2 rods, 5 units). Demonstrate $225 \div 40$ by posing the question: If 40 people need to share 225 blocks, are there enough flats (hundreds) for everyone to get a hundred? [*no*] Trade the two flats for rods, and ask students how many rods (tens) you should have in all. [*22*] Are there enough rods (tens) for everyone to get one? [*no*] What does this say about the quotient? [*It will have only one digit.*]

Division Basics

Division and multiplication are related in the same way addition and subtraction are. If you know that 8 + 6 = 14, then it follows that 14 − 6 = 8. It is the same for division and multiplication. If 3 x 5 = 15, then it follows that 15 ÷ 5 = 3.

Let's say you have 6 units and you want to share them evenly with a friend. This would be written as 6 ÷ 2 or 6/2. To construct the problem, lay out all six units in front of you and divide them between you and your friend one by one. You will see that you each get 3 units.

Let's try it with a larger number. Say you have 2 rods, 4 units and you want to share them among 4 people. Two rods cannot be divided between 4 people, so you have to exchange the rods for units. Portioning the units into 4 groups, you get 6 units per person. It would look something like this:

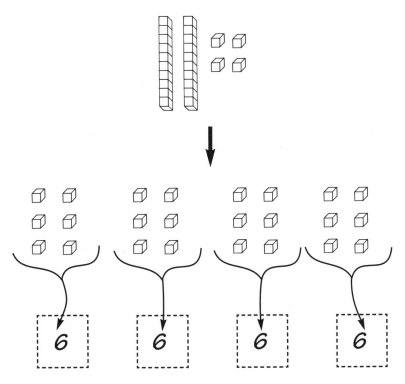

Try sharing a few groups on your own. Fill in the correct numbers for the division sentence, as well as the answer when you've found it. The first one has been done as an example.

1.   You have 2 rods, 5 units to share among 5 people.   _____25_____ ÷ __5__ = __5__

2.   You have 4 rods, 6 units to share among 2 people.   _____ ÷ _____ = _____

3.   You have 3 rods, 6 units to share among 9 people.   _____ ÷ _____ = _____

4.   You have 7 rods, 2 units to share among 8 people.   _____ ÷ _____ = _____

5.   You have 5 rods, 6 units to share among 7 people.   _____ ÷ _____ = _____

Practice Dividing

Tom asked Jake to help him out of a jam. Tom had 4 flats, 7 rods, and 1 unit that he wanted to share evenly between himself and 2 friends. The problem was he couldn't figure out how many blocks each person should get.

Exchanges

Flats	Rods	Units
1		

Flats	Rods	Units
1	5	

Flats	Rods	Units
1	5	7

Jake said, "Let's look at the situation.

You have

Flats	Rods	Units
4	7	1

There are 4 flats. We can give 1 flat to each person. That uses 3 flats."

1 flat per person x 3 people = 3 flats

Flats	Rods	Units
4	7	1
3		
1	7	1

"If we exchange the 1 flat that remains for rods, there will be 17 rods."

Flats	Rods	Units
0	17	1

"We can give each person 5 rods."

5 rods per person x 3 people = 15 rods.

Flats	Rods	Units
0	17	1
	15	
	2	1

"If we exchange the 2 rods that remain for units, there will be 21 units."

Flats	Rods	Units
0	0	21

"Then, each person gets 7 units."

7 units per person x 3 people = 21 units

Practice Dividing

Tom said, "Thanks, Jake. Now I know that each person receives

Flats	Rods	Units
1	5	7

As I was watching you, I realized that we could do this in a single chart. Watch."

Share	1	5	7
3	Flats	Rods	Units
	4	7	1
	3		
	1	7	1
		17	1
		15	
		2	1
			21

"I start with the fact that each person gets 1 flat. I record this on top.
This uses 3 flats, leaving

Flats	Rods	Units
1	7	1

"Now, we'll exchange flats for rods. Each person can have 5 rods (which we record above). That uses up 15 rods, leaving

Flats	Rods	Units
0	2	1

"Exchanging the rods for units, each person can now have 7 units. That uses up all my blocks. I'll record 7 on top."

Share and Share Alike

Tom has some more blocks to share. Help him decide how many each person should get in these situations.

1.

Share			
4	Flats	Rods	Units
	6	3	2

2.

Share			
6	Flats	Rods	Units
	7	0	2

3.

Share			
6	Flats	Rods	Units
	8	2	2

4.

Share			
5	Flats	Rods	Units
	6	7	5

5.

Share				
8	Cubes	Flats	Rods	Units
	8	9	6	8

6.

Share				
3	Cubes	Flats	Rods	Units
	3	6	5	7

Sharing Base Ten Blocks

Now that you know how to make exchanges to divide numbers, let's see what happens if you don't have enough blocks to share even after you make an exchange.

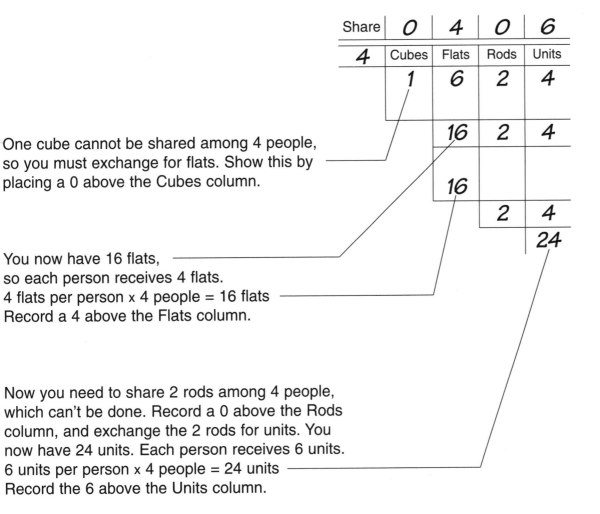

Share	0	4	0	6
4	Cubes	Flats	Rods	Units
	1	6	2	4
		16	2	4
		16		
			2	4
				24

One cube cannot be shared among 4 people, so you must exchange for flats. Show this by placing a 0 above the Cubes column.

You now have 16 flats, so each person receives 4 flats.
4 flats per person x 4 people = 16 flats
Record a 4 above the Flats column.

Now you need to share 2 rods among 4 people, which can't be done. Record a 0 above the Rods column, and exchange the 2 rods for units. You now have 24 units. Each person receives 6 units.
6 units per person x 4 people = 24 units
Record the 6 above the Units column.

So, if you cannot share after making a trade, you put a zero over the column.

More Practice Dividing

Try these problems, but watch out for zeroes. Sometimes they pop up!

1.
Share				
5	Cubes	Flats	Rods	Units
	1	5	3	5

2.
Share				
9	Cubes	Flats	Rods	Units
	1	8	5	4

3.
Share				
8	Cubes	Flats	Rods	Units
	1	5	2	0

4.
Share				
3	Cubes	Flats	Rods	Units
	4	5	3	3

5.
Share				
7	Cubes	Flats	Rods	Units
	7	3	5	7

6.
Share				
6	Cubes	Flats	Rods	Units
	3	6	4	2

How Many?

Tom wants to know if the method Jake showed him will work when he needs to share with more than ten people. Jake has worked it out for him:

Three cubes cannot be shared evenly among 15, so we need to trade them for flats.

We now have 36 flats. Each person receives 2 flats. Record that on the top of the chart over the Flats column. 2 flats per person x 15 people = 30 flats. We are left with 6 flats, 7 rods, 5 units.

We exchange the flats for rods. This gives us 67 rods, which gives each person 4 rods. 4 rods per person x 15 people = 60 rods. Record a 4 over the Rods column. We now have 7 rods, 5 units left.

We exchange the rods for units. This gives us 75 units. When 75 units are shared among 15 people, each person receives 5 units. 5 units per person x 15 people = 75 units. Record the 5 above the Units column on the chart.

Share		2	4	5
15	Cubes	Flats	Rods	Units
	3	6	7	5
		36	7	5
		30		
		6	7	5
			67	5
			60	
			7	5
				75

We see that each person gets 2 flats, 4 rods, 5 units.

Try a few problems on your own.

1.

Share				
23	Cubes	Flats	Rods	Units
	8	1	4	2

2.

Share				
19	Cubes	Flats	Rods	Units
	8	8	7	3

3.

Share				
36	Cubes	Flats	Rods	Units
	6	0	8	4

4.

Share				
32	Cubes	Flats	Rods	Units
	6	5	6	0

Fractions and Decimals

Teaching Notes

The exercises in this section help students understand the concept of fractions and decimals as parts of a whole.

Some students may have problems distinguishing between numerators and denominators. Write several fractions on the blackboard, all with 100 as the denominator. Have students model the fractions using a flat (100) as their base (or denominator) and placing rods and units on top of the flat to show the numerator. Remind them that all the numerators are on top of the denominator, just like in a written fraction.

If students have trouble with place value for tenths, hundredths, and thousandths, you can adapt the place value mat (master on page 95) for decimals by changing the headings.

Introducing Fractions

A fraction represents a part of a whole or a set. A fraction is made of a denominator (the bottom number) and a numerator (the top number). The denominator shows how many equal parts there are to the whole, and the numerator shows how many parts are represented by the fraction.

For example, if you have a set of 4 units and 3 of the units are inside a circle, the circled units represent $\frac{3}{4}$ of the set. The unit outside the circle represents $\frac{1}{4}$ of the set.

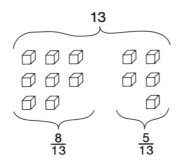

The denominator in each fraction is 4, because you have a total of 4 units in the set. The numerator is either 3 or 1, representing the part of the whole you are trying to show.

> **Remember:** A fraction whose numerator and denominator are the same always equals 1.

Let's look at another example.

Here, we have a set of 13 units, but 5 units have been set aside. The whole set can be written as $\frac{13}{13}$. The part of the whole that has been set aside is $\frac{5}{13}$, and the part of the whole that is left is $\frac{8}{13}$.

You can see the same concept expressed with flats and rods.

1 flat = 10 rods

So 1 rod = $\frac{1}{10}$ of the flat. Place 10 rods side by side to make a flat. If you take 1 rod away from the rest, you have taken away $\frac{1}{10}$ of the flat and left $\frac{9}{10}$ of the flat.

Writing Fractions

For each of the following sets, identify the fraction that is circled and the fraction that is not. The first one has been done for you.

1.

Circled ___$\frac{3}{5}$___   Not circled ___$\frac{2}{5}$___

2.

Circled _____   Not circled _____

3.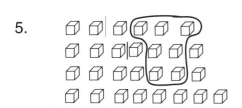

Circled _____   Not circled _____

4.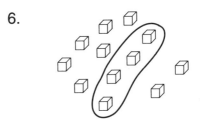

Circled _____   Not circled _____

5.

Circled _____   Not circled _____

6.

What fraction of the set is circled? _____
What is the denominator in this fraction? _____
What is the numerator in this fraction? _____

7.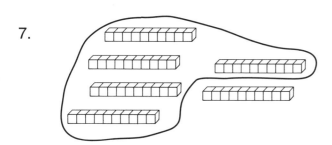

If each rod equals 1, what fraction of the set is circled? _____
If each rod equals 10, what fraction of the set is circled? _____

Writing Fractions

8.

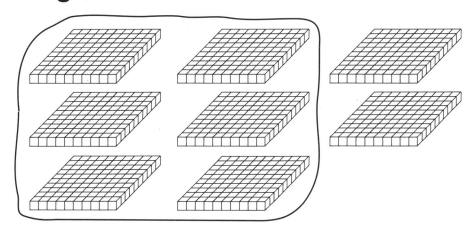

If each flat equals 1, what fraction of the set is circled? _____
If each flat equals 100, what fraction of the set is circled? _____

9.

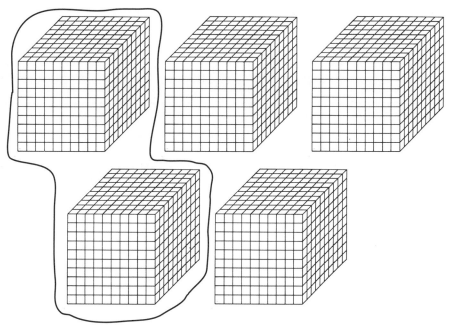

If each cube equals 1, what fraction of the set is circled? _____
If each cube equals 1,000, what fraction of the set is circled? _____

10.

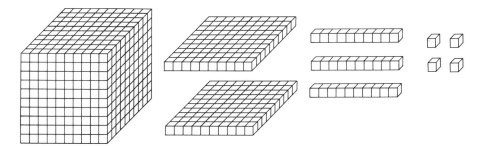

If each of the blocks equals 1, what fraction of the set is the cube? _____
What fraction are the flats? _____
What fraction are the rods? _____
What fraction are the units? _____

Simplifying Fractions

Lisa and Josh were using blocks to write fractions. Lisa wondered whether there was more than one way to write the same fraction. She asked Josh to look at the following set of units:

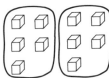

"There are 5 units in each circle and 10 units total," Josh said. "So, each group is $\frac{5}{10}$ of the whole."

"Yes, but the units are broken up into 2 equal groups," Lisa explained. "So, if we say there are 2 groups total, each group is $\frac{1}{2}$ of the whole."

"That's the same as dividing both the 5 and the 10 in $\frac{5}{10}$ by 5," said Josh. "It would look like this."

$$\frac{5}{10} = \frac{5 \div 5}{10 \div 5} = \frac{1}{2}$$

Both of them liked this idea. "Let's see if it will work with any other fractions," Lisa suggested.

> **Remember:** You can make an equivalent fraction by multiplying or dividing both the numerator and denominator by the same number until you get the lowest common denominator.

Help Josh and Lisa simplify the following fractions. Use your blocks to help you see where you can divide further. The first fraction has been done for you.

1. $\dfrac{4}{12} = \dfrac{1}{3}$

2. $\dfrac{5}{40} = $ _____

3. $\dfrac{4}{40} = $ _____

4. $\dfrac{12}{16} = $ _____

5. $\dfrac{24}{32} = $ _____

6. $\dfrac{50}{75} = $ _____

7. $\dfrac{20}{64} = $ _____

8. $\dfrac{72}{104} = $ _____

9. $\dfrac{160}{280} = $ _____

10. $\dfrac{500}{5,000} = $ _____

Introducing Decimals

Another way to describe parts of a whole is with decimals.

Let a 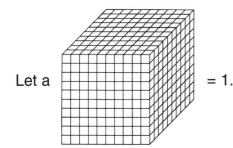 = 1.

Since 10 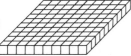 = 1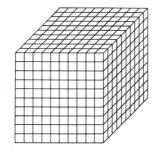

we say each 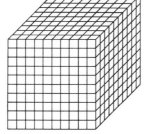 is one of 10 needed, so each flat is $\frac{1}{10}$ or 0.1 of a cube.

Since 100 ⌑⌑⌑⌑⌑⌑ = 1

we say each ⌑⌑⌑⌑⌑⌑ is one of 100 needed, so each rod is $\frac{1}{100}$ or 0.01 of a cube.

Since 1,000 ⬦ = 1

we say each ⬦ is one of 1,000 needed, so each unit is $\frac{1}{1000}$ or 0.001 of a cube.

Keep these ideas in mind as you try to answer the questions on the next page. Use your blocks to help.

Decimals and Fractions

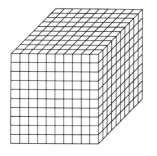

Cube = 1
(one)

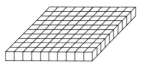

Flat = 1/10 = 0.1
(one tenth)

Rod = 1/100 = 0.01
(one hundredth)

Unit = 1/1,000 = 0.001
(one thousandth)

Fill in the equivalent numbers in the sentences below. The first two are done for you.

1.   0.3 is the same as ___30___ hundredths.

2.   0.3 is the same as ___300___ thousandths.

3.   0.32 is the same as _____ thousandths.

4.   3.2 is the same as _____ tenths.

5.   6.3 is the same as _____ tenths.

6.   6.3 is the same as _____ hundredths.

7.   0.4 is the same as _____ hundredths.

8.   0.4 is the same as _____ thousandths.

9.   5.2 is the same as _____ thousandths.

10.   1.50 is the same as _____ tenths.

11.   0.90 is the same as _____ tenths.

12.   0.230 is the same as _____ hundredths.

13.   0.200 is the same as _____ tenths.

14.   0.123 is the same as 1 tenth + 1 hundredth + _____ thousandths.

15.   0.34 is the same as 2 tenths + _____ hundredths.

16.   2.5 is the same as 1 ones + _____ hundredths.

17.   3.80 is the same as 3 ones + 7 tenths + _____ hundredths.

18.   0.64 is the same as 5 tenths + _____ hundredths.

19.   1.06 is the same as _____ tenths + _____ hundredths.

68

Expanding Decimal Numbers

Cube

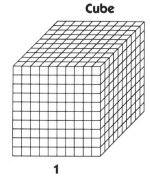

1

Flat

1/10 = 0.1

Rod

1/100 = 0.01

Unit

1/1,000 = 0.001

The number 2.325 is built with:

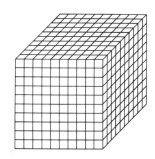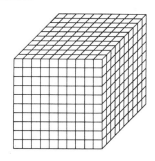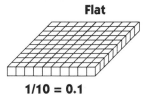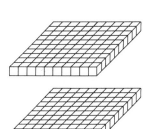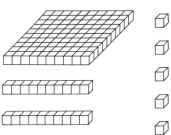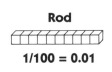

Here are three different ways 2.325 can be written:

2.325 = 2 cubes + 3 flats + 2 rods + 5 units

or

2.325 = 2 ones + 3 tenths + 2 hundredths + 5 thousandths

or

2.325 = (2 x 1) + (3 x 1/10) + (2 x 1/100) + (5 x 1/1,000)

The number 1.206 is built with:

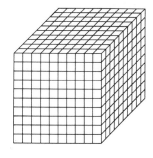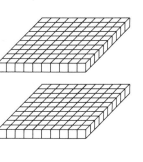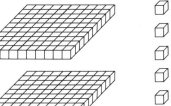

1.206 = _____ cube(s) + _____ flat(s) + _____ rod(s) + _____ unit(s)

or

1.206 = _____ one + _____ tenths + _____ hundredths + _____ thousandths

or

1.206 = (_____ x 1) + (_____ x 1/10) + (_____ x 1/100) + (_____ x 1/1,000)

Build the following numbers yourself. Record three different ways of writing each number.

3.4	2.03	1.235	0.647	3.069
1.938	0.234	1.072	0.307	2.001

Adding and Subtracting Decimals

You can use your blocks to help you add and subtract decimals in the same way you add and subtract whole numbers. Just remember these four simple steps:

1. Line up your places by lining up the decimal points (make sure tenths are with tenths, hundredths are with hundredths, and thousandths are with thousandths).
2. Always work from the smallest to the largest place.
3. Trade and regroup blocks as needed.
4. Fill in zeroes as place holders as needed.

Try these addition problems first. Build the numbers, then find the sums.
The first one has been done for you.

1. 1.35 + 2.06 = _3.41_

$$\begin{array}{r} 1.35 \\ +\ 2.06 \\ \hline 3.41 \end{array}$$

2. 1.3 + 0.365 = _____

$$\begin{array}{r} 1.300 \\ +\ 0.365 \\ \hline \end{array}$$

3. 0.47 + 0.56 = _____

4. 0.704 + 1.056 = _____

5. 2.36 + 0.007 = _____

6. 0.963 + 0.32 = _____

7. 1.481 + 0.359 = _____

8. 0.58 + 1.034 = _____

Now let's try some subtraction problems. Build the original number first and make whatever exchanges are necessary to keep your place values lined up. The first one is done for you.

1. 3.256 – 1.347 = _____

$$\begin{array}{r} 3.256 \\ -\ 1.347 \\ \hline 1.909 \end{array}$$

2. 3.23 – 1.75 = _____

3. 0.563 – 0.374 = _____

4. 1.45 – 0.39 = _____

5. 1.673 – 1.34 = _____

6. 0.278 – 0.045 = _____

7. 2.346 – 1.19 = _____

8. 2.32 – 1.405 = _____

Measurement

Teaching Notes

Base Ten Blocks can be used as both standard and nonstandard units of measure to help children understand that given dimensions, such as length, can be measured in different ways.

Begin with estimating and comparing length in nonstandard units (blocks), then move to measuring length, perimeter, area, and volume using standard units (centimeters). Explain that many things—blocks, paper clips, erasers, and so on—can be used as units of measure.

Review metric measurement—centimeters and decimeters—emphasizing that 10 centimeters (units) equal 1 decimeter (rod).

When calculating perimeter, students may forget to add all sides. Have them label each side of the figures on page 73 to help them keep track.

If students are having trouble estimating length, have them draw lines that are 3 centimeters, 7 centimeters, and 10 centimeters long without using blocks. Then have them measure each line against a rod to see how accurate they were.

To relate perimeter and area more closely, have the class draw their own figures to measure. Instruct students to draw four (closed) figures on a piece of paper, using rods to make straight lines with even numbers of centimeters. Collect the sheets and redistribute them randomly. Have students write their names at the top of the paper and then find the length of each side, the perimeter, and the area for each figure.

To What Lengths Can You Go?

Length is a measure of distance, as from one end of your classroom to the other or from the tip of your pencil to the eraser.

You can estimate the length of something or measure it against something else. For example, place a rod on the desk in front of you. Now place a pencil next to it. Which is longer? Did you need to measure them with a ruler to decide which was longer?

Look at the following pictures and estimate how long each one is in units. Write your answer in the box on the left. Next, measure each picture using a rod (each unit on the rod equals 1 centimeter) and record your answer on the right.

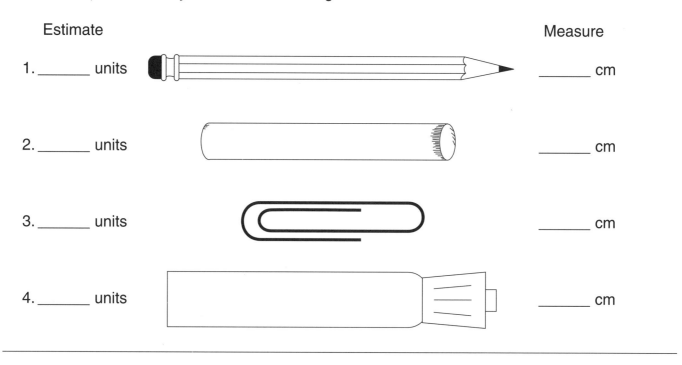

Estimate   Measure

1. _____ units   _____ cm

2. _____ units   _____ cm

3. _____ units   _____ cm

4. _____ units   _____ cm

Classroom Lengths

This exercise is for groups of three or four students. Your teacher will give each group four objects. Write the names of the objects in the chart below. Take turns estimating and measuring the length of each object (use rods to measure).

	Estimate	Object	Measure
1.	Units		cm
2.	Units		cm
3.	Units		cm
4.	Units		cm

When everyone has filled in their charts, compare your answers. Did you all get the same measurements? If not, measure again together.

Finding Your Way Around Perimeters

Perimeter is the distance around a figure. You find the perimeter of a figure by adding up the length of each of its sides.

Find the perimeter of these shapes by lining up units around the outlines of each shape. Each unit = 1 centimeter. The first one has been done for you.

1.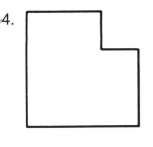

$$\begin{array}{r} 4 \\ 3 \\ 2 \\ 2 \\ 2 \\ +\ 1 \\ \hline 14 \end{array}$$

The perimeter is 14 centimeters (or 14 cm).

> **Remember:** To include the unit measurement (cm) in your answer!

2.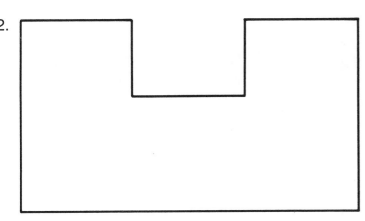

3.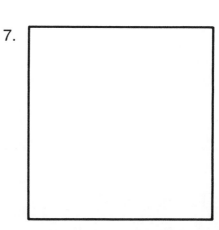

4.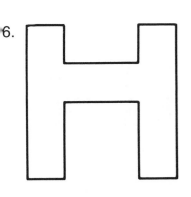

5.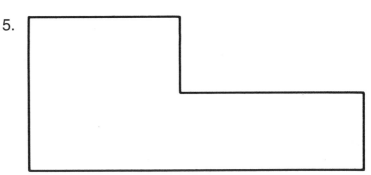

6.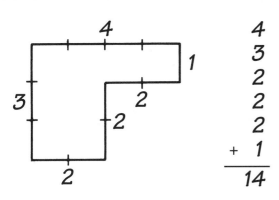

7.

Covering Area

Area is the space a figure covers. Remember that area is always measured in square units. We use an exponent 2 (^{2}) to show square units. For example, cm^2 is used for area.

Aaron found some tiles and wants to know their area. Use the units, which are 1 centimeter on each side, to determine the area of each tile. The smallest one has been done as an example.

1 cm   1 cm

1 cm

The area of this tile is 2 cm^2.

Tile 1 = _____

Tile 2 = _____

Tile 3 = _____

Tile 4 = _____

Covering Area

Tile 5 = _____

Tile 6 = _____

1. Can you find a shortcut for finding area? _____
2. Do you need to count by covering the figure with units? _____
3. State a formula you can use: _____

Extras for Experts

1. Aaron wants to buy 6 tiles just like Tile 2. The store sells them for $1.20 per square centimeter. How much will it cost? _____
2. Courtney wants 4 tiles like Tile 4 and 3 tiles like Tile 6. How much will it cost her at $1.20 per square centimeter? _____

Pump Up the Volume

Volume is the amount of space a figure occupies. Volume is measured in cubic units. We use the exponent 3, (³) to show cubic units. For example cm³ is used for volume

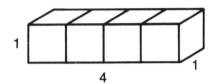 = 1 cubic centimeter = 1 cm³ = 1 x 1 x 1

= 4 cubic centimeters = 4 cm³ = 1 x 4 x 1

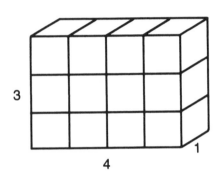 = 12 cubic centimeters = 12 cm³ = 3 x 4 x 1

Volume is determined by multiplying Length x Width x Height:

Build figures with the following measurements, then determine their volume.

1.   Length = 5; width = 2; height = 3   Volume = _____

2.   Length = 4; width = 8; height = 2   Volume = _____

3.   Length = 6; width = 3; height = 4   Volume = _____

4.   Length = 2; width = 8; height = 3   Volume = _____

5.   Length = 9; width = 8; height = 4   Volume = _____

6.   Length = 10; width = 5; height = 3   Volume = _____

7.   Length = 12; width = 10; height = 4   Volume = _____

8.   Length = 8; width = 10; height = 5   Volume = _____

Answer Key

Units, Units, Units, page 6-7

1. 12 units   1 rod, 2 units   2. 17 units   1 rod, 7 units

3. 23 units   1 rod, 13 units   4. 28 units   1 rod, 18 units
             2 rods, 3 units   2 rods, 8 units

5. 34 units   1 rod, 24 units   6. 37 units   1 rod, 27 units
             2 rods, 14 units   2 rods, 17 units
             3 rods, 4 units   3 rods, 7 units

Trading Rods and Units, pages 8-9

1. START WITH 33 UNITS

Number of Exchange	Now Have		Total Number of Units Exchanged
	Rods	Units	
1	1	23	10
2	2	13	20
3	3	3	30

2. START WITH 56 UNITS

Number of Exchange	Now Have		Total Number of Units Exchanged
	Rods	Units	
1	1	46	10
2	2	36	20
3	3	26	30
4	4	16	40
5	5	6	50

3. START WITH 65 UNITS

Number of Exchange	Now Have		Total Number of Units Exchanged
	Rods	Units	
1	1	55	10
2	2	45	20
3	3	35	30
4	4	25	40
5	5	15	50
6	6	5	60

4. START WITH 79 UNITS

Number of Exchange	Now Have		Total Number of Units Exchanged
	Rods	Units	
1	1	69	10
2	2	59	20
3	3	49	30
4	4	39	40
5	5	29	50
6	6	19	60
7	7	9	70

5. START WITH 87 UNITS

Number of Exchange	Now Have		Total Number of Units Exchanged
	Rods	Units	
1	1	77	10
2	2	67	20
3	3	57	30
4	4	47	40
5	5	37	50
6	6	27	60
7	7	17	70
8	8	7	80

6. START WITH 48 UNITS

Number of Exchange	Now Have		Total Number of Units Exchanged
	Rods	Units	
1	1	38	10
2	2	28	20
3	3	18	30
4	4	8	40

Trading Rods and Units, pages 8-9

7. START WITH 50 UNITS

Number of Exchange	Now Have		Total Number of Units Exchanged
	Rods	Units	
1	1	40	10
2	2	30	20
3	3	20	30
4	4	10	40
5	5	0	50

At the Toy Shop, page 10

1. 5; 0; 5; 0 dimes, 5 pennies

2. 7; 0; 7; 0 dimes, 7 pennies

3. 52; 4; 52; 5 dimes, 2 pennies

4. 17; 1; 17; 1 dime, 7 pennies

Units and Rods, page 11

Units Started With	Total Number of Units Exchanged	Now Have	
		Rods	Units
16	10	1	6
38	30	3	8
54	50	5	4
47	40	4	7
67	60	6	7
83	80	8	3
90	90	9	0
46	40	4	6
85	80	8	5
93	90	9	3
79	70	7	9

Keep It Rolling, page 12

1. 1

2. 6

3. 2 rolls; 5, 5; 6, 4; no

4. 10 rolls; 1

5. 1, 3, 6 or 1, 4, 5 or 2, 2, 6 or 2, 3, 5 or 2, 4, 4 or 3, 3, 4

6. 1, 1, 4, 4 or 1, 1, 3, 5 or 1, 1, 2, 6 or 1, 2, 2, 5 or 1, 2, 3, 4 or 1, 3, 3, 3 or 2, 2, 2, 4 or 2, 2, 3, 3

7. 1, 1, 1, 1, 6 or 1, 2, 1, 1, 5 or 1, 3, 1, 1, 4 or 2, 2, 1, 1, 4 or 2, 2, 2, 1, 3 or 2, 2, 2, 2, 2 or 3, 2, 1, 1, 3

Counting Backward, page 13-14

1. START WITH 5 RODS, 8 UNITS

Number of Exchange	Total Number of Rods Exchanged	Now Have	
		Rods	Units
1	1	4	18
2	2	3	28
3	3	2	38
4	4	1	48
5	5	0	58

2. START WITH 4 RODS, 9 UNITS

Number of Exchange	Total Number of Rods Exchanged	Now Have	
		Rods	Units
1	1	3	19
2	2	2	29
3	3	1	39
4	4	0	49

3. START WITH 7 RODS, 1 UNIT

Number of Exchange	Total Number of Rods Exchanged	Now Have	
		Rods	Units
1	1	6	11
2	2	5	21
3	3	4	31
4	4	3	41
5	5	2	51
6	6	1	61
7	7	0	71

4. START WITH 6 RODS, 0 UNITS

Number of Exchange	Total Number of Rods Exchanged	Now Have	
		Rods	Units
1	1	5	10
2	2	4	20
3	3	3	30
4	4	2	40
5	5	1	50
6	6	0	60

5. START WITH 8 RODS, 3 UNITS

Number of Exchange	Total Number of Rods Exchanged	Now Have	
		Rods	Units
1	1	7	13
2	2	6	23
3	3	5	33
4	4	4	43
5	5	3	53
6	6	2	63
7	7	1	73
8	8	0	83

Meet the Flat, page 15

1. yes; 10

2. 10; 9 rods, 10 units; 8 rods, 20 units

3. 10 rods

4. 10 rods; 100 units

Total Number of Rods Exchanged	Now Have	
	Rods	Units
1	9	10
2	8	20
3	7	30
4	6	40
5	5	50
6	4	60
7	3	70
8	2	80
9	1	90
10	0	100

Let's Make a Trade, page 16-17

1. START WITH 22 RODS

Number of Exchange	Now Have		Total Number of Rods Exchanged
	Flats	Units	
1	1	12	10
2	2	2	20

3. START WITH 71 RODS

Number of Exchange	Now Have		Total Number of Rods Exchanged
	Flats	Rods	
1	1	61	10
2	2	51	20
3	3	41	30
4	4	31	40
5	5	21	50
6	6	11	60
7	7	1	70

2. START WITH 63 RODS

Number of Exchange	Now Have		Total Number of Rods Exchanged
	Flats	Rods	
1	1	53	10
2	2	43	20
3	3	33	30
4	4	23	40
5	5	13	50
6	6	3	60

4. START WITH 89 RODS

Number of Exchange	Now Have		Total Number of Rods Exchanged
	Flats	Rods	
1	1	79	10
2	2	69	20
3	3	59	30
4	4	49	40
5	5	39	50
6	6	29	60
7	7	19	70
8	8	9	80

Let's Make a Trade, page 16-17

5. START WITH 45 RODS

Number of Exchange	Now Have		Total Number of Rods Exchanged
	Flats	Rods	
1	1	35	10
2	2	25	20
3	3	15	30
4	4	5	40

6. START WITH 50 RODS

Number of Exchange	Now Have		Total Number of Rods Exchanged
	Flats	Rods	
1	1	40	10
2	2	30	20
3	3	20	30
4	4	10	40
5	5	0	50

Trading Practice, page 19

START WITH 256 UNITS

Number of Exchange	Now Have			Total Number of Units Exchanged	Total Number of Rods Exchanged
	Flats	Rods	Units		
1	0	1	246	10	0
2	0	2	236	20	0
3	0	3	226	30	0
4	0	4	216	40	0
5	0	5	206	50	0
6	0	6	196	60	0
7	0	7	186	70	0
8	0	8	176	80	0
9	0	9	166	90	0
10	0	10	156	100	0
11	1	0	156	100	10
12	1	1	146	110	10
13	1	2	136	120	10
14	1	3	126	130	10
15	1	4	116	140	10
16	1	5	106	150	10
17	1	6	96	160	10
18	1	7	86	170	10
19	1	8	76	180	10
20	1	9	66	190	10
21	1	10	56	200	10
22	2	0	56	200	20
23	2	1	46	210	20
24	2	2	36	220	20
25	2	3	26	230	20
26	2	4	16	240	20
27	2	5	6	250	20

Number Patterns, page 20

Number of Units to Start With	Exchange for Rods Now Have		Exchange for Flats Now Have		
	Rods	Units	Flats	Rods	Units
275	27	5	2	7	5
463	46	3	4	6	3
782	78	2	7	8	2
603	60	3	6	0	3
526	52	6	5	2	6
419	41	9	4	1	9
378	37	8	3	7	8
487	48	7	4	8	7
136	13	6	1	3	6
283	28	3	2	8	3

Exchange for flats

Save the Day!, page 21

Number of Units	Total Number of Units Exchanged	Total Number of Rods Exchanged	Now Have		
			Flats	Rods	Units
35	30	0	0	3	5
235	230	20	2	3	5
143	140	10	1	4	3
367	360	30	3	6	7
450	450	40	4	5	0
549	540	50	5	4	9
307	300	30	3	0	7
630	630	60	6	3	0
98	90	0	0	9	8
182	180	10	1	8	2
43	40	0	0	4	3
596	590	50	5	9	6

Conversions, page 22

Number of Units	Flats	Rods	Units
45	0	4	5
99	0	9	9
35	0	3	5
321	3	2	1
903	9	0	3
400	4	0	0
563	5	6	3
89	0	8	9
657	6	5	7
835	8	3	5
198	1	9	8
387	3	8	7
742	7	4	2
946	9	4	6
849	8	4	9

Meet the Cube, page 23

1. yes
2. 10; 10; 1
3. 9 flats, 10 rods
4. 10 flats; 100 rods

Complete this chart:

Total Number of Flats Exchanged	Now Have	
	Flats	Rods
1	9	10
2	8	20
3	7	30
4	6	40
5	5	50
6	4	60
7	3	70
8	2	80
9	1	90
10	0	100

Exchanging Flats, page 24-25

1. START WITH 24 FLATS

Number of Exchange	Now Have		Total Number of Flats Exchanged
	Cubes	Flats	
1	1	14	10
2	2	4	20

Exchanging Flats, page 24-25

2. START WITH 67 FLATS

Number of Exchange	Now Have		Total Number of Flats Exchanged
	Cubes	Flats	
1	1	57	10
2	2	47	20
3	3	37	30
4	4	27	40
5	5	17	50
6	6	7	60

3. START WITH 39 FLATS

Number of Exchange	Now Have		Total Number of Flats Exchanged
	Cubes	Flats	
1	1	29	10
2	2	19	20
3	3	9	30

4. START WITH 81 FLATS

Number of Exchange	Now Have		Total Number of Flats Exchanged
	Cubes	Flats	
1	1	71	10
2	2	61	20
3	3	51	30
4	4	41	40
5	5	31	50
6	6	21	60
7	7	11	70
8	8	1	80

5. START WITH 48 FLATS

Number of Exchange	Now Have		Total Number of Flats Exchanged
	Cubes	Flats	
1	1	38	10
2	2	28	20
3	3	18	30
4	4	8	40

7. START WITH 70 FLATS

Number of Exchange	Now Have		Total Number of Flats Exchanged
	Cubes	Flats	
1	1	60	10
2	2	50	20
3	3	40	30
4	4	30	40
5	5	20	50
6	6	10	60
7	7	0	70

6. START WITH 53 FLATS

Number of Exchange	Now Have		Total Number of Flats Exchanged
	Cubes	Flats	
1	1	43	10
2	2	33	20
3	3	23	30
4	4	13	40
5	5	3	50

Let's Trade, page 26

START WITH 135 RODS

Number of Exchange	Now Have			Total Number of Units Exchanged	Total Number of Rods Exchanged
	Flats	Rods	Units		
1	0	1	125	10	0
2	0	2	115	20	0
3	0	3	105	30	0
4	0	4	95	40	0
5	0	5	85	50	0
6	0	6	75	60	0
7	0	7	65	70	0
8	0	8	55	80	0
9	0	9	45	90	0
10	0	10	35	100	10
11	1	0	35	100	10
12	1	1	25	110	10
13	1	2	15	120	10
14	1	3	5	130	10

Erased!, page 27

Number of Rods Started With	Total Number of Rods Exchanged	Total Number of Flats Exchanged	Now Have		
			Cubes	Flats	Rods
46	40	0	0	4	6
324	320	30	3	2	4
234	230	20	2	3	4
278	270	20	2	7	8
368	360	30	3	6	8
637	630	60	6	3	7
506	500	50	5	0	6
740	740	70	7	4	0
273	270	20	2	7	3
54	50	0	0	5	4
596	590	50	5	9	6
458	450	40	4	5	8

Complete the Chart, page 28

Start with this number of units	Exchange for Rods Now Have		Exchange for Flats Now Have			Exchange for Cubes Now Have			
	Rods	Units	Flats	Rods	Units	Cubes	Flats	Rods	Units
1,364	136	4	13	6	4	1	3	6	4
2,375	237	5	23	7	5	2	3	7	5
1,693	169	3	16	9	3	1	6	9	3
2,390	239	0	23	9	0	2	3	9	0
3,457	345	7	34	5	7	3	4	5	7
1,409	140	9	14	0	9	1	4	0	9
4,372	437	2	43	7	2	4	3	7	2
2,437	243	7	24	3	7	2	4	3	7
634	63	4	6	3	4	0	6	3	4
4,361	436	1	43	6	1	4	3	6	1

Construct These Numbers, page 29

Number of Units	Cubes	Flats	Rods	Units
1,345	1	3	4	5
299	0	2	9	9
3,275	3	2	7	5
1,321	1	3	2	1
804	0	8	0	4
3,700	3	7	0	0
2,654	2	6	5	4
498	0	4	9	8
1,078	1	0	7	8
3,568	3	5	6	8
924	0	9	2	4
1,196	1	1	9	6
2,837	2	8	3	7
2,310	2	3	1	0
3,247	3	2	4	7

Greater Than, Less Than, or Equal To?, page 30

2. right

4. equal

6. right

3. left

5. right

7. equal

All in the Bottom, page 32

2. 4, 2, 6

3. 7, 2, 9

Fact Rectangles, page 33

1. 3, 5, 8; No exchanges

2. 8, 6, 14; yes, 1 rod, 4 units

3. 4, 7, 11; yes, 1 rod, 1 unit

Combine Collections, page 34

	Cubes	Flats	Rods	Units
Kyle	1	4	6	3
Ashley	3	8	2	7
Total	4	12	8	10
Exchanges	1		1	
Total After Exchange	5	2	9	0

Check the Totals, page 36

1.

Cubes	Flats	Rods	Units
6		6	

2.

Cubes	Flats	Rods	Units
9			

3. Ok as is

Find the Total, page 37

1.

Name	Cubes	Flats	Rods	Units
Kyle	5	7	9	6
Ashley	2	4	7	8
Total	7	11	16	14
Total After Exchange	8	2	7	4

2.

Name	Cubes	Flats	Rods	Units
Kyle	3	1	6	8
Ashley	5	7	3	9
Total	8	8	9	17
Total After Exchange	8	9	0	7

3.

Name	Cubes	Flats	Rods	Units
Kyle	4	5	9	7
Ashley	1	8	6	4
Total	5	13	15	11
Total After Exchange	6	4	6	1

4.

Name	Cubes	Flats	Rods	Units
Kyle	3	1	8	4
Ashley	6	2	3	5
Total	9	3	11	9
Total After Exchange	9	4	1	9

Practice Combining the Blocks, page 38

1.

	Cubes	Flats	Rods	Units
	3	6	9	4
	2	8	5	7
Total	5	14	14	11
Total After Exchange	6	5	5	1

2.

	Cubes	Flats	Rods	Units
	3	5	7	6
	2	3	4	9
Total	5	8	11	15
Total After Exchange	5	9	2	5

3.

	Cubes	Flats	Rods	Units
	6	5	8	7
	2	4	8	6
Total	8	9	16	13
Total After Exchange	9	0	7	3

4.

	Cubes	Flats	Rods	Units
	5	3	7	6
	3	6	1	5
Total	8	9	8	11
Total After Exchange	8	9	9	1

5.

	Cubes	Flats	Rods	Units
	7	8	4	6
	1	8	4	6
Total	8	16	8	12
Total After Exchange	9	6	9	2

6.

	Cubes	Flats	Rods	Units
	6	3	9	2
	1	5	4	7
Total	7	8	13	9
Total After Exchange	7	9	3	9

More Practice Combining the Blocks, page 39

1.

	Cubes	Flats	Rods	Units
	5	7	6	8
	3	1	2	4
Total	8	8	8	12
Total After Exchange	8	8	9	2

2.

	Cubes	Flats	Rods	Units
	3	9	8	5
	2	4	6	7
Total	5	13	14	12
Total After Exchange	6	4	5	2

3.

	Cubes	Flats	Rods	Units
	8	2	8	5
	1	3	9	5
Total	9	5	17	10
Total After Exchange	9	6	8	0

4.

	Cubes	Flats	Rods	Units
	4	9	7	4
	3	8	7	6
Total	7	17	14	10
Total After Exchange	8	8	5	0

More Practice Combining the Blocks, page 39

5.

	Cubes	Flats	Rods	Units
	6	7	9	3
	4	8	2	6
Total	10	15	11	9
Total After Exchange	11	6	1	9

6.

	Cubes	Flats	Rods	Units
	5	8	6	1
	4	7	3	9
Total	9	15	9	10
Total After Exchange	10	6	0	0

Addition Practice, page 40

1.
```
  2 8 3 5
  5 9 6 8
  1 1 1
  8 8 0 3
```

2.
```
  7 9 8 4
  1 8 9 7
  1 1 1
  9 8 8 1
```

3.
```
  3 8 4 6
  2 6 9 7
  1 1 1
  6 5 4 3
```

4.
```
  8 7 4 6
  1 2 4 8
      1
  9 9 9 4
```

5.
```
  4 6 7 8
  5 8 9 6
  1 1 1
 10 5 7 4
```

6.
```
  5 3 4 0
  2 9 4 7
  1
  8 2 8 7
```

7.
```
  3 4 0 5
  8 9 4 5
  1   1
 12 3 5 0
```

8.
```
  4 1 8 6
  6 8 3 6
  1 1 1
 11 0 2 2
```

Don't Go Broke!, page 42

Spin 1—BANK

	Rods	Units
Started	10	
Bank	3	2
Left	6	8

Spin 2—GIVE

	Rods	Units
Started	6	8
Give	1	6
Left	5	2

Spin 3—TAKE

	Rods	Units
Started	5	2
Take	5	3
Left	10	5

Spin 4—GIVE

	Rods	Units
Started	10	5
Give	4	6
Left	5	9

Spin 5—BANK

	Rods	Units
Started	5	9
Bank	4	3
Left	1	6

More "Don't Go Broke!", page 43

JEFF

Spin 6—BANK

	Rods	Units
Started	7	9
Bank	3	6
Left	4	3

Spin 7—TAKE

	Rods	Units
Started	4	3
Take	2	6
Left	6	9

Spin 8—BANK

	Rods	Units
Started	6	9
Bank	4	4
Left	2	5

Spin 9—GIVE

	Rods	Units
Started	2	5
Give	3	1
Left		4

LIZ

Spin 6—TAKE

	Rods	Units
Started	1	6
Take	4	5
Left	6	1

Spin 7—TAKE

	Rods	Units
Started	6	1
Take	3	1
Left	9	2

Spin 8—GIVE

	Rods	Units
Started	9	2
Give	2	4
Left	6	8

Spin 9—BANK

	Rods	Units
Started	6	8
Bank	1	6
Left	5	2

Jeff goes broke in Spin 9.

Don't Go Flat Broke!, page 44

Spin 3—GIVE

	Flats	Rods	Units
Started	9	2	3
Give	3	8	1
Left	5	4	2

Spin 4—TAKE

	Flats	Rods	Units
Started	5	4	2
Take	2	5	7
Left	7	9	9

1.

Jeff	Flats	Rods	Units
Started	8	5	2
Bank	3	7	4
Left	4	7	8

2.

Liz	Flats	Rods	Units
Started	6	4	8
Give	5	9	3
Left	0	5	5

3.

Jeff	Flats	Rods	Units
Started	3	8	5
Take	4	3	7
Left	8	2	2

4.

Liz	Flats	Rods	Units
Started	5	8	1
Bank	3	7	9
Left	2	0	2

Raising the Stakes, page 45

Spin 3—BANK

	Cubes	Flats	Rods	Units
Started	9	2	0	9
Bank	4	1	3	7
Left	5	0	7	2

Spin 4—TAKE

	Cubes	Flats	Rods	Units
Started	5	0	7	2
Take	3	2	6	8
Left	8	3	4	0

1.

Jeff	Cubes	Flats	Rods	Units
Started	6	9	6	3
Bank	4	4	8	5
Left	2	4	7	8

2.

Liz	Cubes	Flats	Rods	Units
Started	7	5	3	7
Give	4	4	8	2
Left	3	0	5	5

3.

Jeff	Cubes	Flats	Rods	Units
Started	7	4	9	6
Take	2	5	4	8
Left	10	0	4	4

4.

Liz	Cubes	Flats	Rods	Units
Started	5	6	9	2
Give	4	4	8	9
Left	1	2	0	3

Borrowing, page 46

1.

	Cubes	Flats	Rods	Units
	6	6	15	15
Start	6	7	6	5
Give	4	3	9	7

2.

	Cubes	Flats	Rods	Units
	4	12	16	10
Start	5	3	7	0
Give	4	8	9	4

3.

	Cubes	Flats	Rods	Units
	4	13	6	11
Start	5	3	7	1
Give	4	8	4	9

4.

	Cubes	Flats	Rods	Units
	3	9	12	10
Start	4	0	3	0
Give	2	2	8	7

5.

	Cubes	Flats	Rods	Units
	6	15	14	14
Start	7	6	5	4
Give	4	9	6	8

6.

	Cubes	Flats	Rods	Units
	5	14	9	14
Start	6	5	0	4
Give	2	9	3	8

7.

	Cubes	Flats	Rods	Units
	8	8	11	10
Start	8	9	2	0
Give	3	6	5	1

8.

	Cubes	Flats	Rods	Units
	6	13	17	16
Start	7	4	8	6
Give	3	6	8	9

What Remains, page 47

2.

Cubes	Flats	Rods	Units
7	15	14	3
8̸	6̸	4̸	3
− 5	7	8	2
2	8	6	1

3.

Cubes	Flats	Rods	Units
6	14	16	13
7̸	5̸	7̸	3̸
− 3	6	7	7
3	8	9	6

4.

Cubes	Flats	Rods	Units
5	10	6	14
6̸	0̸	7̸	4̸
− 4	8	5	8
1	2	1	6

5.

Cubes	Flats	Rods	Units
5	16	10	7
6̸	7̸	0̸	7
− 4	8	9	4
1	8	1	3

6.

Cubes	Flats	Rods	Units
6	11	15	15
7̸	2̸	6̸	5̸
− 5	3	9	8
1	8	6	7

7.

Cubes	Flats	Rods	Units
5	6	9	10
5	7̸	0̸	0̸
− 4	3	8	2
1	3	1	8

8.

Cubes	Flats	Rods	Units
7	9	16	16
8̸	0̸	7̸	6̸
− 6	2	7	8
1	7	9	8

9.

Cubes	Flats	Rods	Units
3	10	3	17
4̸	0̸	4̸	7̸
− 2	9	3	8
1	1	0	9

10.

Cubes	Flats	Rods	Units
4	12	10	5
5̸	3̸	0̸	5
− 3	8	4	5
1	4	6	0

Find the Value, page 48

1. 2,078
3. 3,898
5. 2,873
7. 4,333
9. 1,689

2. 2,891
4. 1,327
6. 2,887
8. 1,725
10. 4,540

Let's Multiply, page 50

1. 15
2. 96
3. 150
4. 200
5. 938
6. 702
7. 836
8. 858

Multiplying by 10, 100, and 1,000, page 51

1. 70
2. 450
3. 2,400
4. 2,000
5. The product of multiplying a number by 10, 100, or 1,000 is the number with the corresponding number of zeroes added on.

Multiplying with Pete, page 52-53

1. 3 flats, 9 rods, 6 units
2. 15 flats, 37 rods, 20 units
   or 18 flats, 9 rods
3. 24 flats, 38 rods, 10 units
   or 27 flats, 9 rods
4. 35 flats, 19 rods, 2 units
   or 36 flats, 9 rods, 2 units

Division Basics, page 55

2. $46 \div 2 = 23$
3. $36 \div 9 = 4$
4. $72 \div 8 = 9$
5. $56 \div 7 = 8$

Share and Share Alike, page 58

1. 158
2. 117
3. 137
4. 135
5. 1,121
6. 1,219

More Practice Dividing, page 60

1. 307
2. 206
3. 190
4. 1,511
5. 1,051
6. 607

How Many?, page 61

1. 354
2. 467
3. 169
4. 205

Writing Fractions, page 64-65

2. $\frac{6}{15}$; $\frac{9}{15}$
3. $\frac{3}{19}$; $\frac{16}{19}$
4. $\frac{15}{25}$; $\frac{10}{25}$
5. $\frac{7}{28}$; $\frac{21}{28}$
6. $\frac{4}{12}$; 12; 4
7. $\frac{5}{6}$; $\frac{50}{60}$
8. $\frac{6}{8}$; $\frac{600}{800}$
9. $\frac{2}{5}$; $\frac{2000}{5,000}$
10. $\frac{1}{10}$; $\frac{2}{10}$; $\frac{3}{10}$; $\frac{4}{10}$

Simplifying Fractions, page 66

2. $\frac{1}{8}$
3. $\frac{1}{10}$
4. $\frac{3}{4}$
5. $\frac{3}{4}$
6. $\frac{2}{3}$
7. $\frac{5}{16}$
8. $\frac{9}{13}$
9. $\frac{4}{7}$
10. $\frac{1}{10}$

Decimals and Fractions, page 68

3. 320
4. 32
5. 63
6. 630
7. 40
8. 400
9. 5,200
10. 15
11. 9
12. 23
13. 2
14. 13
15. 14
16. 150
17. 10
18. 14
19. 10; 6

Expanding Decimal Numbers, page 69

1.206 = 1 cube + 2 flats + 0 rods + 6 units
       = 1 one + 2 tenths + 0 hundredths + 6 thousandths
       = (1 x 1) + (2 x 1/10) + (0 x 1/100) + (6 x 1/1,000)

3.4   = 3 cubes + 4 flats
      = 3 ones + 4 tenths
      = (3 x 1) + (4 x 1/10)

2.03 = 2 cubes + 0 flats + 3 rods
      = 2 ones + 0 tenths + 3 hundredths
      = (2 x 1) + (0 x 1/10) + (3 x 1/100)

Expanding Decimal Numbers, page 69

1.235 = 1 cube + 2 flats + 3 rods + 5 units
     = 1 one + 2 tenths + 3 hundredths + 5 thousandths
     = (1 x 1) + (2 x 1/10) + (3 x 1/100) + (5 x 1/1,000)

0.647 = 0 cubes + 6 flats + 4 rods + 7 units
     = 0 ones + 6 tenths + 4 hundredths + 7 thousandths
     = (0 x 1) + (6 x 1/10) + (4 x 1/100) + (7 x 1/1,000)

3.069 = 3 cubes + 0 flats + 6 rods + 9 units
     = 3 ones + 0 tenths + 6 hundredths + 9 thousandths
     = (3 x 1) + (0 x 1/10) + (6 x 1/100) + (9 x 1/1,000)

1.938 = 1 cube + 9 flats + 3 rods + 8 units
     = 1 one + 9 tenths + 3 hundredths + 8 thousandths
     = (1 x 1) + (9 x 1/10) + (3 x 1/100) + (8 x 1/1,000)

0.234 = 0 cubes + 2 flats + 3 rods + 4 units
     = 0 ones + 2 tenths + 3 hundredths + 4 thousandths
     = (0 x 1) + (2 x 1/10) + (3 x 1/100) + (4 x 1/1,000)

1.072 = 1 cube + 0 flats + 7 rods + 2 units
     = 1 one + 0 tenths + 7 hundredths + 2 thousandths
     = (1 x 1) + (0 x 1/10) + (7 x 1/100) + (2 x 1/1,000)

0.307 = 0 cubes + 3 flats + 0 rods + 7 units
     = 0 ones + 3 tenths + 0 hundredths + 7 thousandths
     = (0 x 1) + (3 x 1/10) + (0 x 1/100) + (7 x 1/1,000)

2.001 = 2 cubes + 0 flats + 0 rods + 1 unit
     = 2 ones + 0 tenths + 0 hundredths + 1 thousandth
     = (2 x 1) + (0 x 1/10) + (0 x 1/100) + (1 x 1/1,000)

Adding and Subtracting Decimals, page 70

Addition

2. 1.665	3. 1.03
4. 1.76	5. 2.367
6. 1.283	7. 1.84
8. 1.614	

Subtraction

2. 1.48	3. 0.189
4. 1.06	5. 0.333
6. 0.233	7. 1.156
8. 0.915	

To What Lengths Can You Go?, page 72

1. 10 cm	2. 7 cm
3. 5 cm	4. 9 cm

Finding Your Way Around Perimeters, page 73

2. 32 cm	3. 22 cm
4. 12 cm	5. 26 cm
6. 22 cm	7. 20 cm

Covering Area, page 74-75

Tile 1 = 10 cm^2
Tile 2 = 21 cm^2
Tile 3 = 45 cm^2
Tile 4 = 52 cm^2
Tile 5 = 48 cm^2
Tile 6 = 40 cm^2

1. Multiply the shortest side by the longest side.
2. no
3. side x side = cm^2

Extras for Experts
1. $151.20
2. $393.60

Pump Up the Volume, page 76

1. 30 cm^3	2. 64 cm^3
3. 72 cm^3	4. 48 cm^3
5. 288 cm^3	6. 150 cm^3
7. 480 cm^3	8. 400 cm^3

Place Value Mat Copy Master

HUNDREDS	TENS	ONES

Game Spinner Copy Master

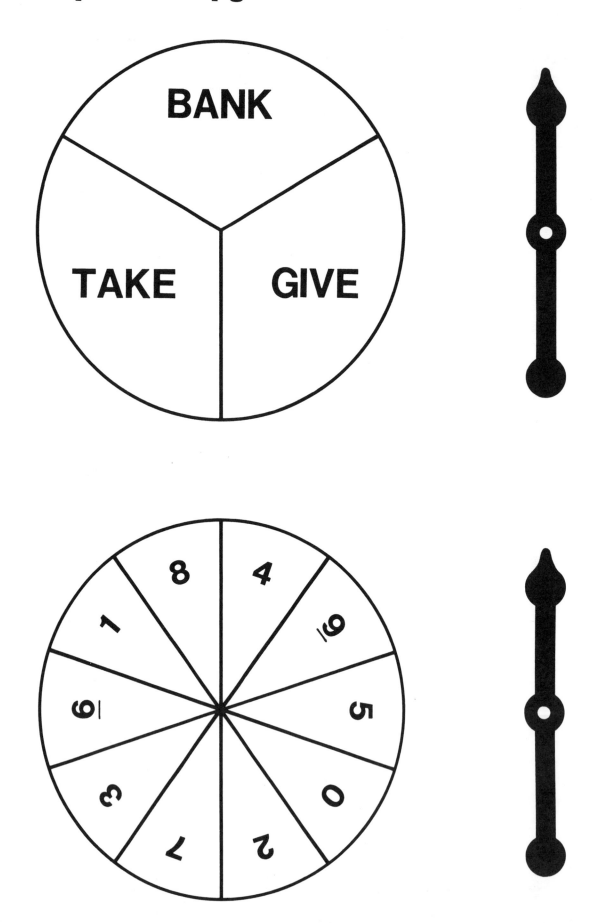